AI for Everyone:

Benefitting from and building trust in the technology

Jiro Kokuryo, Keio University.
Catharina Maracke, Keio University.
Toby Walsh, UNSW Sydney, Data61 & TU Berlin.

Published by

AI Access

AI Access is a not-for-profit publisher with a highly respected scientific board that publishes open access monographs and collected works. Our text are available electronically for free and in hard copy at close to cost. We welcome proposals for new texts.

ISBN 978-0-244-55730-0

AI Access
Managing editor: Toby Walsh
URL: `aiaccess.org`

Contents

Chapter 1

Introduction:
Jiro Kokuryo, Catharina Maracke and
Toby Walsh

This book has been created as a result of a discussion series organized by the Association of Pacific Rim Universities (APRU) which was financially supported by Google. Statements and opinions expressed are those of the authors and under their full responsibility.

1.1 Project Overview

If governed adequately, AI (artificial intelligence) has the potential to benefit humankind enormously. However, if mismanaged, it also has the potential to harm humanity catastrophically. Drawing upon this realization, the Association of Pacific Rim Universities (APRU) with the support of Google, launched an international collaborative research project in 2017. The Association of Pacific Rim Universities is a consortium of 50 leading research universities in 17 economies of the Pacific Rim. Formed in 1997, APRU fosters collaboration between member universities, researchers, and policymakers contributing to economic, scientific and cultural advancement in the Pacific Rim.

The project started with a call for papers, which resulted in the submission of twelve working papers (see Table 1 for the list of authors and titles). Two drafts were made for each paper, which received feedback from other members ("coaches"). Completion of these was scheduled for the end of November 2018. The present report is based on the second draft, submitted for the brush-up session held at Hong Kong University of Science and Technology on September 1, 2018.

The first meeting of all contributors was held at Keio University on December 1st 2017. Over the course of the discussions, all contributors agreed that the title of the project should be "AI for everyone: benefitting from and building trust in the technology". This title reflects the belief that "access to the benefits of

AI, awareness about the nature of the technology, governance of the technology and its development process with a focus on responsible development, should be transparent, open, understood by and accessible to all people regardless of their geographic, generational, economic, cultural and/or other social background."

Four sources of societal threats that need to be addressed were identified to which analyses and suggestions were offered by the academics.

1. **"Black box" machines manipulating human society:** Technical solutions to enable humans to understand, explain, trust and control the behavior of AI, reducing their perception as " black boxes" were offered. As well, a framework for the development of a certification system for trustworthy AI systems was proposed.

2. **Unethical uses of AI:** Moral, technical and legal solutions to the malicious unethical use of AI were discussed. The importance of responsibility of "moral agents" for the use of AI in war and political manipulation was explored. A proposal was offered to update the notion of legal culpability.

3. **New threats on privacy:** The dangers of inference attacks in identifying and learning patterns in data to predict attributes of subjects or databases were identified. Suggested technical solutions were made including ways to integrate data scattered across various organizations while protecting the privacy of individuals. A philosophical and historical overview of the tension between individual and collective benefits of managing data was provided.

4. **AI may widen the gap between the rich and the poor:** The prospect of the "replacement of human beings" by AI was discussed along with a strategy to educate and re-educate the new and existing workforces to equip them to deal with the emerging needs.

While many of the issues and analyses are global and universal in scope, some distinctly regional characteristics have emerged throughout the discussion process. A particularly important divide seems to exist in attitudes toward individualism and autonomy, which are perceived and institutionalized in various ways, giving rise to different attitudes toward the use of technology in state surveillance for public order. In response, a policy statement calling for sensitivity to political and cultural diversity has been put together (see later).

1.2   Executive summary

AI will have a major impact on society. This statement is no longer in question and is consistently reflected across all twelve papers submitted to the "AI for Everyone Project." The current discussion, however, is driven by the notion of whether this impact will be positive or negative. While analyzing possible consequences for different stake-holders, all papers identify and engage with a very practical yet deeply philosophical common theme around the notions of individuality and autonomy, or in perhaps more compelling terms, authority and responsibility for decisions made by machines.

In thinking about this, we must begin with a recognition that much of modern civilization derived by the West has been dependent on an assumption that autonomous individual humans are taking control of, and responsibilities for, consequences of using artifacts. Sustainability of this assumption, however, is under question, particularly in an Asian context that has different philosophical traditions.

Humans will increasingly depend on the judgment of AI, which relies on a vast accumulation of data provided by networked computers. Who is to be held responsible for the accidents caused by autonomously driven cars is a commonly raised question, to which the traditional assumption of autonomous individual human beings does not provide a suitable answer. Protection of individual human rights, including the right to privacy, has become an increasingly complex endeavor as people take advantage of other people's data in many aspects of their lives, including for medical needs. While technical solutions probably exist, we have not yet been able to define what it is that we want to protect.

A venture into the essence of person-hood leads us to an interesting proposition, that of recognizing machines as "personalities," at least in a legal sense (as we already legally recognize corporations as pseudo-persons). Assuming automated decisions can be attributed to "AI" personalities or institutions, such an arrangement would sound attractive to engineers fearful of being held responsible for all the consequences of AI, including the unintended ones. However, we must emphasize that while acknowledging the increasing popularity of the idea, none of the contributors supported it in the end to avoid evasion of responsibility by others in cases of malicious use of technology.

The notion of machine personality also raises the question of moral agency. Whether or not to allow AI driven weapons to attack people is a real and immediate moral issue we have at hand.

Humans are a heterogeneous species. We must be sensitive to the diversity among cultures, particularly when thinking about the relationship between individuals and communities. The hasty imposition of conventional ethics and standards can cause resentment among the imposed and societal conflicts as new forms of networked communities supported by machine intelligence emerge.

Perhaps less fundamental than the issue of autonomy, but also consistently discussed was the concept of "trust." While there are multiple facets that can be discussed around the concept of trust, two aspects seem especially important. First, humans are wondering if and to what extent technology can be trusted. Second, engineers are wondering what kind of "explainability" they should build into the system so that humans can trust the system.

The concept of trust is characterized by the willingness to rely on another party's actions. When it comes to the relationship between humans and technology, it seems critical for humans to have at least some level of understanding of the technology in order to "trust" and take advantage of the enormous technological opportunity in front of us. At the same time, it seems equally important to build a common understanding of the possible social impacts when building the technology. Thus, technology and new systems should not be developed in isolation but in close communication with other disciplines and perspectives. Put another way, we as a society should think carefully about education, training, and governance for technology development.

In the sea of uncertainties surrounding our future relationship with AI, one thing seems very clear. That is, we must be prepared to work beyond traditional discipline borders to rethink the fundamental elements of our civilization and boldly work together to navigate the technology so that it benefits our future. We must also be prepared to find an adequate response for those who are concerned about malicious uses of the technology.

1.3 Summaries and Analyses of Individual Papers

This section offers an overview of the submitted working papers, which have been structured around the four issues identified as societal threats in the context of this project. Some of the authors have chosen to publish their papers within this volume. Others have or will publish them elsewhere in the peer reviewed literature.

Fear of "black box" machines manipulating human society

Unlike traditional information systems that essential operate using predetermined algorithms, much of AI's behavior depends on the data that it learns from and is not transparent to the users. Papers have been written on this subject from both a technical standpoint to identify and solve the problem as well as from a behavioral perspective, analyzing how humans may in fact be manipulated. Delegation of monitoring to others, such as experts, by means of certification may also provide a solution.

Lim (2018) discusses the importance of "explainable artificial intelligence," which allows end users to understand the models and algorithms at work in systems, leading to better control. To this end, the author developed a framework of explanation layers that addresses the question of why people make certain inquiries and what the main goals for explanations should be. Methodologies on how to provide explanations were developed based on the stated goals. People's cognitive limitations are analyzed to propose a "user-centric explainable AI" that reduces decision errors by users (in this paper, medical professionals).

Singh (2018) discusses the prospect of increasing human trust in machines by providing a model-agnostic and intuitive way to explain any machine learning algorithm. Successful development of such a method would allow humans to understand the behavior of AI, reducing their perception as "black boxes." The paper focuses on the explainability of classification models, on providing interpretable descriptions of how input affects predictions. It also sets goals in providing "local" explanations of why a specific decision was made for a specific instance. Three forms of explanations, namely linear models, anchors (sufficient conditions), and counter examples are introduced. Illustrative applications of these three forms are provided.

Gal (2018), taking on the case of Replika, offers empirical evidence on how human users of chatbots can build emotional attachments to the pseudo-personalities AI generate. By using a variation of the Uses and Gratifications Theory to guide a structured content analysis, the author analyzed 447 user reviews of the application. The analysis indicates that using Replika is a largely gratifying experience, especially when looking for artificial companionship. It also finds, however, that engagement in this artificial companionship can negatively affect the users, both emotionally and socially. Implications of this "artificial socialization" are discussed alongside a call for continued study of the topic.

Yap (2018) offers a framework for the development of a certification system for trustworthy AI systems. The author identifies such issues around AI as: (1) how to show that the results are correct or accurate, (2) how to explain and make interpretations on the results, and (3) how to show that the results are fair. The author then explores how people can put their trust in technology under such limitations, concluding that to be trusted, systems have to (a) be developed by trustworthy developers, (b) be fair, and (c) generate understandable results. They also need to be secure, even in an adversarial environment, and come with assurances. "Certification elements" are proposed to develop a certification system to increase trustworthiness. Such proposed certification elements should be designed to include technical expertise as well as neutrality in their evaluation. Another option presented is to allow self- certification, relying on disclosure by system providers.

Recognition that AI may be put to unethical uses and that some restraining mechanisms are necessary

Malicious, unethical use of AI can be catastrophic to human existence. This part of the project studies moral, technical, and legal solutions to this problem. Analysis is focused on specific contexts, such as war and political manipulation, using online robots. More fundamental questions around responsibility are also explored from the perspective of criminal law.

Erskine (2018) focuses particularly on conflict situations, namely war, to argue the importance of the notion of "moral agents" for "moral restraints." Moral agents are defined as "actors that possess capacities for understanding and reflecting upon moral requirements, and for acting in such a way as to conform to them." Comparing flesh-and-blood humans, corporations (institutions), and AI, only humans (and institutions, to the extent individual humans can be held accountable for them) have the quality of being "moral patients" vulnerable to suffering from a breach of morals by others. Given that robots lack this quality, it seems appropriate for humans to be the ultimate moral agent. The author points out two kinds of risks involved in allowing non-flesh-and-blood agents to be moral agents as follows: (1) abdicating responsibility to non-moral agents and (2) eliding the responsibilities of distinct moral agents.

Monroy et al. (2018) reviews the literature on - and offers views on - bot detection mechanism. Botnets can be used to provoke trending topics and have been proven to be effective in either favoring political figures, misrepresenting said figures' opponents, or influencing voting behavior. Therefore, detection of botnets is of high importance. Bot detection on Twitter is based on the premise that genuine client accounts show different behavior to bot or semi-automated accounts. By analyzing combinations of tweet content, sentiment, tweet account, account usage, and social network features, detecting the existence of botnets becomes possible. The authors take a contrast pattern-based approach to detecting botnets. They are also testing a "generative adversarial network" approach. Results are forthcoming.

Dremliuga (2018) questions the future viability of our present day criminal law framework. The spread of social systems where humans and AI coexist increases the ambiguity surrounding intentionality and culpability in harmful events. Hence, criminal law systems that focus on penalizing responsible individuals may become neither fair nor effective at preventing harm. The author moves on to discuss the practicality of giving legal person-hood to machines in a manner analogous to corporate person-hood. While recognizing increasing support for the idea, the author questions its effectiveness, as it may fail to penalize and deter the malicious use of technology. In conclusion, the author proposes a revision of the concept of culpability, suggests increased control of the possession of powerful AI systems, and opposes the adoption of the machine person-hood concept.

New attacks on privacy

There is a new risk of inference attack on privacy, i.e., there may be breaches of privacy through AI analyzing the results of predictions to determine attributes of subjects or databases. While privacy has been an issue from the early days of Internet use, the issue is taking on a new and more serious character given AI's great power of inference. That is, by identifying and learning patterns in data, machines are capable of "mining" sensitive private information from data and/or even from results of the predictions generated by other systems. A philosophical revisiting of the notion of the individual is also necessary for a more fundamental understanding of the meaning of the emerging term "panopticon."

Shokri (2018) points out the dangers of "inference attacks," i.e., breaches of privacy resulting from AI analyzing the results of predictions to determine the attributes of subjects or databases. The author then seeks algorithms to minimize the threat of inference attacks while maximizing predictive capabilities of AI at work. This is done by introducing a "regularizing" function designed to prevent the predictive model from over-fitting. Experiments were conducted using adversarial inference attack models to test the effectiveness of the concept.

Yang and Chen (2018) explore ways to integrate data that is scattered across various organizations while protecting the privacy of the individuals. The authors propose three types of implementations, namely (1) transfer learning, (2) federated learning, and (3) federated transfer learning, where "transfer" involves the transfer of knowledge (not data) and "federated" refers to integrating data on the same subject in different parts of the schemas. The authors point out data waste in the conventional federated approach and recommend a federated transfer learning approach.

Lau (2018) explores the notion of individuality in the context of AI, seemingly providing a contemporary realization of "panopticon," or a system of governance by ubiquitous social surveillance. The author discusses how the West has been developing the concept of the individual's freedom as a human right, but quickly adds that a recognition of resulting conflict among the interests of the individuals has brought about a notion of "disciplining of individuality." The idea of panopticon emerged in this context with the goal of providing maximum surveillance with the least effort. Both governments and large commercial online services are in a position to play the role of the "inspector" and are becoming a contemporary threat to the notion of individuality. The difference between the current and the nineteenth century context is that nowadays, people are often the beneficiaries of such surveillance, leading them to be willing participants. The invisibility of surveillance is also a characteristic of contemporary times. Thus, the all-encompassing data system neither suppresses nor controls any individual, but it dissolves individuals into a new collectivism that is made up not of individuals but of something more fundamental than humans. We may be heading into an age of post-humanism or transhumanism.

Fear that AI may widen the gap between the rich and the poor

Changes in the world of work and especially loss of jobs has been one of the primary concerns in the context of discussing AI. While fear of job loss is nothing new in the interaction between technology and society, AI's flexibility in performing highly contextual work adds a whole new dimension to the problem.

Tobar (2018), with "replacement of humans" as an underlying theme, identifies two lines of developmental philosophies for AI. One pushes AI researchers to concentrate on examining whether machines can have a mind (Babbage approach). The other focuses on the replacement of humans by AI while recognizing the impossibility of artificially creating a mind (Cartesian approach). The author states that this categorization is in line with Searle's distinction between strong and weak AI. Weak AI researchers have shown that "weak AI has not been as weak as was originally thought." While a rule-based approach has limits, machine learning can result in machines simply replacing human labor.

Shen (2018) focuses on people born in or before the 1990s in China, as they are considered less trained in AI-related fields and thus highly susceptible to technological advances in the job market. The author provides empirical evidence of a trend toward increasing wages and a labor force shift in China between 1978 and 2016, coinciding with the introduction of computers and automated machinery. Given this evidence, the author proposes a list of college majors that need to incorporate computer science education, and provides an assessment outline for the design of AI courses offered by both colleges and corporations.

1.4   Policy statement

The participants drew up the following policy statement pulling together the many valuable conversations that were had during the course of the project.

- AI (artificial intelligence) has the potential to benefit humankind enormously if it is governed adequately. However, it also has the potential to harm humanity catastrophically if it is mismanaged.

- This message, coming from the Pacific Rim Universities, particularly emphasizes the need for sensitivity to the diversity in culture, religion, and political systems when developing governance philosophies and structures.

- Governments, academia, businesses, and non-profit organizations must work together across cultural and political boundaries to establish trust in technology, both by adequately managing the technology and by enabling people to use the technology to beneficial ends.

- The Association of Pacific Rim Universities, with its members coming from a diverse range of political and cultural backgrounds but united behind its academic rigor, offers a unique platform for open discussions.

- In this project, aimed at building a community of researchers on the beneficial use of AI, we have been successful in agreeing on a common goal, that is, access to the benefits of AI, awareness about the nature of the technology, governance of the technology, and its development process with a focus on responsible development should be transparent, open, understood by, and accessible to all people regardless of their geographic, generational, economic, cultural, and/or other social background.

- We have also identified the following major issues to be addressed:
    - Fear of "black box" machines manipulating human society
    - Recognition that AI may be put to unethical uses and that some restraining mechanism are necessary
    - Risk of inference attack on privacy, i.e., breach of privacy through AI analyzing the results of predictions to determine attributes of subjects or databases
    - Fear that AI may widen the gap between the rich and the poor

- AI is likely to change the foundational constructs of human society, such as autonomy, ownership, and markets. While using conventional norms to manage immediate issues, we must be prepared to think out of the box to offer alternatives regarding the future of humanity.

- While the research is still very much preliminary, we are actively pursuing opportunities to interact with policymakers, businesses, and leaders in society to exchange ideas based on substantial scientific evidence and constructs that reflect history and cutting-edge technologies.

Authors and Affiliations	Title	Coaches
Dremliuga, Roman. Far Eastern Federal University	How Development of Artificial Intelligence Technology Will Cause Changes in Crime and Criminal Law	Erskine, Monroy, Lay
Erskine, Toni. Australian National University	Flesh-and-Blood, Corporate, Robotic? Moral Agents of Restraint and the Problem of Misplaced Responsibility in War	Shen, Yap, Dremliuga
Gal, Danit. Peking University/ Keio University	Best Bot Friend (BBF): The Emotional and Social Implications of Socializing with an AI	Yang Shokri, Monroy
Lau, Chong-Fuk. Chinese University of Hong Kong	The Life of Individuality: Modernity, Panopticon, and Dataism	Gal, Tobar, Shokri
Lim, Brian Y. National University of Singapore	Designing Theory-Driven User-Centric Explainable AI	Yap, Yang, Singh.
Monroy, Raul. Tecnologico de Monterrey	Political Bot Detection on Tweets	Dremliuga, Erskine
Singh, Sameer. University of California, Irvine	Explaining Decisions of Black-box AI Models	Lim, Shokri, Yang
Shen, Yifan. Fudan University	AI Education for Everyone: How to Integrate Future Labor Force into Digital Frontier?	Gal, Dremliuga
Shokri, Reza. National University of Singapore	Privacy of Black-box Deep Learning: Analysis and Defense	Monroy, Tobar
Tobar, Felipe. Universidad de Chile	How Weak Has Been Weak Artificial Intelligence? The Unseen Societal Consequences of Machine Learning	Lau, Erskine
Yang, Qiang & Chen, Toby T. Hong Kong University of Science & Technology	Federated Transfer Learning: Building AI for Everyone with Data Protection	Tobar, Yap, Lim
Yap, Roland. National University of Singapore	Toward a Certification Framework for Trustworthy AI Systems	Shen, Singh

Table 1.1: List of working papers

Chapter 2

How development of Artificial intelligence technology will cause changes in crime and criminal law: Roman Dremliuga

2.1 Introduction

The idea of this part is to review a combination of main trends and threats in the fields of implementation of AI and development of criminal law. I apologize to academic lawyers who get used to the fact that any idea of this work should be revealed in a document at least 70 pages long as required by the tradition of scientific writing on jurisprudence. The author tries to avoid complicated and intricate legal reasoning in order to make the text as accessible as possible to a wide range of readers from different subject areas.

Artificial intelligence is a tool to ease daily life. The issue is that for some people crime is their daily life. Criminals always try to use technological advantages to increase economic benefits of crime as well as to be more efficient and successful in committing a crime. Fast boats used by pirates, automobiles - by bank robbers, drones - by drug dealers, and the Internet - by hackers. All are examples of active involving innovations in criminal sphere. Probably there are no exclusions and any new technology may be used both for legal and for illegal purposes. Some people are likely to believe that legal usage is more common, but it is somewhat arguable assumption.

For instance, in case of the Internet, the most of its content is pornography that is illegal for most people of the world (all Muslim states, China, Russia etc.). Moreover, almost 100% of child pornography that is illegal everywhere is distributed through the Internet. In case of some 'special' Internet technologies such as Darknet or anonymizers percent of illegal use often overestimates legal benefits. Darknet, for instance, is the main forum for the illegal drug trade and distribution of illegal information [1] . It seems that some technologies are more natural to be used for illegal purposes even though developers of such technologies were led by noble intentions. Both the Internet and Darknet were created as a tool that facilitates science and technologies, makes people closer, destroys racial, religious and cultural barriers, but in practice the net development had a lot of negative consequences, and one of them is its use by criminals.

The Internet is a very indicative example because it shows that an idealistic anticipation of future use of technology may cause significant problems in future. The Internet occupied the world before clear rules and understanding of future problems appeared although most of problems could be avoided at initial stages of development and introduction of technology. In general, legal rules follow development of technologies and are not prepared for future changes.

Understanding the current and future legal framework is very significant. First of all, law and its enforcement are used to govern a society. It implies that studying of AI from legal perspective allows to understand what challenges to social security caused by wide introduction of autonomous systems. Secondly, for manufacturers of high technology products it is easier to understand what products should not be invested because they are able to assess legal risks.

There are a lot of papers devoted to ethic (and sometimes legal) aspects of AI development and use. Some authors propose introduction of ethical (or legal) rules into AI behavior principals as a universal remedy from harm caused by AI systems. But as Patrick Lin fairly commented on robots with AI *"One natural way to think about minimizing risk of harm from robots is to program them to obey our laws or follow a code of ethics. Of course, this is much easier said than done, since laws can be vague and context-sensitive, which robots may not be sophisticated enough to understand, at least in the foreseeable future"*[2].

Substantial problem of ethical rules is that every state ideology, generation, community of professionals, subcultures has their own system of ethical rules. Sometimes they are totally incompatible with each other and we are not able to discuss ethical system of rules in the singular. Unification of robot legal rules means of unification of legal systems that is principally impossible in the foreseeable future [3].

2.2   Criminal law and AI

Criminal Law is not the same in all countries but it is considered as one of the most efficient social tools for the control of society. Despite differences between states national Criminal Law defends the fundamental rights and freedoms of any society. It regulates and intervenes into social relations in most dangerous and significant cases of misconduct. There are many ways for the governments to control its society, such as moral, economic and cultural. Of note, one of the most efficient measures is criminal law. "Since only criminal law includes significant sanctions, the criminal law is considered the most efficient measure to control individuals. Controlling the individuals through criminal law is legal social control"[4].

The main questions that the author formulates in this essay are the following:

1. How would one be liable for intentional and negligent crimes committed with

use of AI (for instance, developer, trainer or person(s) who contacts with AI) and what are limits of such liability? AI system could be very dangerous for intentional or unintentional unlawful use. For instance, an insane person commands robot to commit some unlawful acts or some criminals intentionally use robot as a tool for offense.

2. Is it possible that some types of AI become so dangerous that it would be prohibited to own or use them in general? There is analogy with a weapon or explosive materials which not every person has permission to use. In most countries you must have a license to own a weapon or explosive. Similarly, children or incapacitated persons are not permitted to use a weapon by the law. For some kind of AI system it would be reasonable. Or governments should develop rules regulating use of artificial intelligence and a system of licensing like with automobile transport. This question concerns criminal law because serious negative consequences of not following rules probably will imply criminal liability (as with transport, for instance, when a drunk driver kills a pedestrian).

3. Is it possible that AI would be recognized as a subject to criminal law (analogy with joint ventures or some animals)?

4. Could we anticipate some kinds of use of AI by criminals?

In other words, this part explores artificial intelligence as: means of committing a crime, a source of heightened danger, a subject of crime, and AI as an accelerator of crime.

In case when we review how the use of artificial intelligence as a tool to commit a crime changes the nature of offense, it may seem that an artificial intelligence system is just a "high-tech gun" but this statement is far from true. Due to high level of autonomy of some existing and developed AI systems[5] as well as to unpredictability of some wide-used algorithms in AI system (for instance, machine learning algorithm)[6] a relation between acts of an offender and harm or risk of real harm caused by the acts is more complicated than with a use of other high technologies. The use of AI influences not only on objective characteristics of committed crime but on subjective (mental) characteristics as well.

In accordance with modern theory of criminal law, except cases of strict liability, any crime to be recognized as such by the court has to have two main elements: actus reus (or physical element of a crime) and mens rea (mental element of a crime). Such terminology is characteristic of countries of common law, but if we analyze the criminal law of countries of statutory law (like China [7], Germany [8], Russia [9] etc.), then there is similar situation.

Lists of acts that are considered to be criminal vary from country to country but they are mostly the same. Among globally recognized crimes are: murder; voluntary manslaughter; larceny; embezzlement; false pretenses; robbery; burglary, forgery etc. The similar situation is with mental element of the crime, as some authors conclude *"Despite the fact that lawyers on both sides of the Atlantic operate with different legal technical terms, criminal culpability rests upon a generally accepted understanding of what constitutes a guilty mind (mens rea), and voluntary conduct"* [10]. Further we will rely mainly on the terminology of

common law countries, sometimes referring to examples from the criminal law of
countries of statutory law.

2.3   The concept of culpability in crime law and AI systems

Mens rea is a culpable state of mind in the individual committing the crime,
usually there are two, three or four modes in criminal law culpability that depend
on particular jurisdiction. For instance, the United States' legal tradition defines
four modes of culpability: purpose, knowledge, recklessness, and negligence that
are reflected in The Model Penal Code (MPC) developed by the American Law
Institute (ALI) [11]. Criminal law of England has three modes: intention (divided
into direct and indirect), recklessness and negligence [12]. Russian Criminal
Code defines four forms of guilt: intent, indirect intent, extreme recklessness
and negligence [13]. The Chinese Penal Code mentions two modes of culpability:
intent and negligence [14] but criminal law has three forms of intent [15].

The question is how issue of forms of guilt is related with crimes committed
with the use of AI. The answer is that an autonomous system as a tool of crime
increases unpredictability and ambiguity of current legal orders. We will try to
clarify this statement further. All mentioned jurisdictions *"deconstruct mens rea
into the cognitive and volitional elements"* [16] and *"the interplay and intensity of
these constitutive elements determine the degree of person's culpability"*. At the
same time Artificial intelligence is recognized as a machine or software that sometimes has wide cognitive abilities (to know, understand, and think) and artificially
autonomous will. As some authors define autonomous machine as *"reactive (it
responds in a timely fashion to changes in the environment), self-controlling (i.e. it
exercises control over its own actions and is not directly controlled by any other
agent), goal-oriented (it does not simply act in response to the environment), and
temporally continuous (it is a continuously running process)"* [17]. Conceptually it
means that degree of person's culpability when AI is a tool of a crime would be
affected by cognitive and volitional characteristics of AI.

Intentional crimes. From the mental element point of view intentional crimes
is the most dangerous kind of crimes. Criminal intent (purpose) implies that a
person foresees and wills the possible negative consequences of his/her conduct.
For instance, if a person uses a gun to kill somebody, it is obvious that most of
the world's adult population (except some tribes who do not have a lot of contacts
with civilization) understand that a result is predictable pushing a trigger of a
pistol and directing it to a victim. Even if a person denies that he/she predicts
and wills a death of a victim, the court would use conception of *virtual certainty*
[18] (in English criminal law or similar conceptions in other jurisdictions) when
probable consequences are obvious for any sane person. Courts around the world
have extensive practice in establishing this form of guilt.

In case when AI is used as a tool of crime the question of culpability becomes
more difficult because of the ability of the artificial intelligence system to make
decisions and to learn depends on the environment in which it operates. For
instance, what would be in case when a person gives command to complicated AI

system that is already able to understand human speech and text as well as able to learn and control its own conduct. Imagine that during its mission AI kills somebody not because intent of operator but as a side-kick effect. Reasonable suggestion is that a person who commands is probably not liable because he/she could not foresee and because he/she does not push trigger, does not choose target etc.

Such point of view could exclude *any* commanders of military robots from any forms of criminal liability. For instance, genocide, the most severe war crime, is a serious violent act *"committed with intent to destroy, in whole or in part, a national, ethical, racial or religious group"* [19]. Some AI systems already demonstrate inclinations to racial prejudice [20] and other biases [21]. Imagine that a commander gives an order to eliminate all enemy combatants to AI robot, but the machine inheriting human biases will prefer as a target people of a specific race. The fact is that in terms of objective consequences in real world it would be serious crime but nobody will be liable because genocide is only an act *"committed with intent"* [22]. There is no genocide formula when a person is guilty of negligence. This hypothetical example demonstrates general idea that intent of a person could be distorted by autonomous cognition and will of AI system and consequences could be very serious.

Special attention we have to pay to predictability of possible negative consequences of conduct in light of crime with purpose (direct intent) mode of culpability. AI system is programmed according to developer/programmer's intent and final user mostly may rely on user's guide or some information from the developer to foresee possible behavior of AI. In case of AI with ability to self-learning behavior is able to be unpredictable as from the developer's point of view as well as from the user's side. Demonstrative example is Tay-bot developed by Microsoft with AI and ability to self-learning [23]. Tay uses statements of users to study how to participate in conversation and as a result acquires some insulting phrases. A big scandal was caused by some Tay pro-Nazi phrases which it was taught by users and transmitted on line. It is reasonable doubts that Microsoft purposely developed AI that would be insulting people in the Internet or that user who asks Tay predicted such insulted answers. As a result nobody is culpable.

This means that the law-enforcer and legislator should reconsider the approach to determining culpability in the case of using artificial intelligence systems for committing intentional crimes. Because AI has own artificial cognition and will, courts could not rely on traditional concept of culpability in intentional crimes. Of particular concern is the use of automated lethal weapon in military operations and local conflicts in the future, since international criminal law has no mechanism of liability for war crimes, crimes against humanity and genocide committed with use of AI. The world community should discuss new rules of criminal prosecution in case of using AI in which it will be possible to take into account the degree of culpability of the commander, developer, machine learning specialist and other responsible persons.

Criminal negligence. Probably a really liable person who is able to influence on harm caused by AI system would be the developer (programmer). If somebody creates autonomous program or robot to intentionally commit some crimes and cause serious harm, it would be intentional crime. But presumably developer would be guilty of negligence that implies that person *"should be aware of a substantial and unjustifiable risk that the material element exists or will result from his conduct. The risk must be of such a nature and degree that the actor's failure to perceive it, considering the nature and purpose of his conduct and the circumstances known to him, involves a gross deviation from the standard of care that a reasonable person would observe in the actor's situation"* [24]. The common formula for negligence in different jurisdictions is that a person is not aware of substantial and unjustifiable risk but he/she ought to be aware.

The most obvious issue that arises from definition of criminal negligence given in Model Penal Code what would be standard of care in terms of AI products development. This area develops so fast that there is no sense to establish such standards. Does it mean that nobody would be liable or that any person who does not take into consideration all potential harm caused by its product would be liable. Both alternatives are unacceptable. If product developers are free from criminal liability, it would lead to dramatic social consequences. Despite programmer still would be civilly liable for the damages caused to victims by his product, if revenue is more than amount of compensation to victims, he will continue to produce dangerous product. The second option is when a person developing AI system has to take into consideration all potential harm caused by the product. The challenge here is that less people will be involved in AI development legally due to unpredictable legal risks.

Due to lack of court practice in the sphere of AI manufacturer's liability to study this issue it is necessary to review approaches of liability of the manufacturer in common. In practice, when the court decides whether the developer is guilty of negligence, it has to establish what measures he has taken to reduce the risks of harm to the consumer. As some authors comment, if we want the developer (manufacturer) to be held liable, *"it can be proven in court that the company was negligent, with regard to the defects, risks, and potential hazards arising from the use of their product, then the company could also be criminally, as well as civilly, liable for the damages caused to victims by their product"* [25]. In areas not related to artificial intelligence there are certain limitations of the manufacturer's liability.

The basic argument of the manufacturer to defend against negligence charges is use of industry standard [26] or special norms. For instance, self-driving car producer has to follow road traffic safety requirements. *If safety requirements in binding law are violated this can constitute a criminal offense, entitling the police to intervene* [27]. Policy when manufacturer follows standards is able to produce collision of social norms. Imagine situation when a child jumps on the road in front of a self-driving car, it has to turn to the oncoming lane to avoid of bumping child. This maneuver violates general safety requirements and if we follow policy of industry standards as base for criminal liability, manufacturer will be guilty of negligence. If car kills or seriously injures child, it would be more socially dangerous but developer would avoid criminal liability. Standards were established to decrease potential harm in general but AI systems can find more optional way to conduct in a specific situation.

It is obvious that manufacturer would be able to save a lot of lives if he does not strictly uphold the law and standards. As a questionnaire that imitates dangerous situations on the road in which an autonomous vehicle is delivered to dangerous situation shows that more people that choose cars with AI have to save lives than follow the law. The examples of dangerous situations provided on the mentioned web-site demonstrate that even for people that are moral beings it is difficult to choose what decision has to be made especially when the choice is complicated by additional parameters of prepositive alternative victims (age, social value, gender etc.) [28]. Who knows what a manufacturer would choose - potential criminal liability or real decreasing of potential harm to society?

Another way for developer to avoid liability for negligent crime is use of notification to consumers. It is enough to notify consumers of a foreseeable risk during use of the product and developer would not be liable. Duty of notification is clarified in national legislations in different ways but has similar content. Consumer has to be informed by producer about serious risk of harm that would be caused by the product. For instance, the General Product Safety Regulations 2005 of the United Kingdom define that *"within the limits of his activities, a producer shall provide consumers with the relevant information to enable them—(a)to assess the risks inherent in a product throughout the normal or reasonably foreseeable period of its use, where such risks are not immediately obvious without adequate warnings, and (b)to take precautions against those risks"* [29]. Predictable challenge here is not only to foresee risk but provide relevant information. As AI is software or hardware that have very complicated system of responding to environment as well this system is dynamic in case of self-learning, it would be difficult to develop adequate notice to the customer.

Special concern is on the fact that products with artificial intelligence become closer to our children. Robo pets, robo care-givers, AI programs for education of infants are not in future. In most national jurisdictions a toy with small details has a label on the package informing that it contains parts that are a choking hazard to young children. But how will producers fulfill a duty to warn. AI system could be so complicated and bring a lot of unpredictable risks.

Systems with the ability to self-learn create additional challenges. In fact, the programmer is able to predict some further risks that will emerge during self-learning of the developed system. But Tay example evidences that not all risks could be predicted. Moreover, somebody could intentionally intervene in the process of AI learning to cause negative consequence. How would the degree of liability of a programmer and a third party be shared?

As Fenwick fairly commented on problem of corporate criminal liability *"punishment without fault or, alternatively, punishment that is disproportionate to the degree of fault is correctly regarded as inappropriate and unjust"* [30]. It implies that courts get a new challenge. If an offender is not recognized all risks in case of using AI but be punished as he do, it would be considered as inappropriate. If owner (commander, designer) is strictly liable for all acts of its AI it would be unfair. As well it would be unfair if owner (commander, designer) avoid criminal liability just point out AI as guilty. As a problem is a relatively new it takes time to find balance between two extremes.

The aim of the above part is to highlight key legal considerations related to the AI and conception of culpability in criminal law. Result of the analysis does not mean that we have to stop development of this promising kind of technology. It just indicates that not simple questions arise in that sphere. This brief overview of how culpability issue becomes more complicated due to AI has more questions than answers but I hope that it provokes future studies. The main challenge which could not be overcome by the traditional theory of criminal law is that AI is "gun" with its own cognition and will.

2.4 Dangerous AI systems

Artificial intelligence systems become more complicated and are used in critical areas as public security, medicine, transportation, military needs etc. When thinking systems will become a common thing, a society will inevitably face the problems of limiting permission for use and possess some kinds of artificial intelligence systems.

There are a lot of things that are prohibited by the criminal law to use, distribute and possess in modern societies. In the majority of jurisdictions, among such things are weapon, explosives, narcotics, counterfeit drugs, nuclear and biohazard materials etc. Practically limitations are different and depend on jurisdiction and type of proscribed items or substances. For instance, in the United States *"whoever knowingly possesses or causes to be present a firearm or other dangerous weapon in a Federal facility (other than a Federal court facility), or attempts to do so, shall be fined under this title or imprisoned not more than 1 year, or both"* [31]. A distributor of weapon has to have a license [32] and refrain from selling, delivering, or otherwise transferring weapon to juvenile [33]. Despite the fact that in the United States the right to bear and keep arms is protected by the Constitution [34], this right has serious limitations. Although in the United States the Second Amendment limits the scope for government regulation, the Bureau of Alcohol, Tobacco, Firearms and Explosives (ATF) [35] exists to do the regulatory enforcement and criminal investigation of gun trafficking cases.

The United States is in the minority of countries that defend the right to have a gun but the majority of counties have stricter rules. For instance, Chinese Criminal Code enshrined that *"whoever illegally manufactures, trades in, transports, mails or stores any guns, ammunition or explosives shall be sentenced to fixed-term imprisonment of not less than three years but not more than 10 years"* [36]. The similar situation exists in Russian criminal law, i.e. in accordance with Article 226 of the Criminal Code of the Russian Federation *"stealing or possession of firearms, their components, ammunition, explosives, or explosive devices shall be punishable by deprivation of liberty for a term of three to seven years"* [37].

In case of other *"dangerous things"* the situation is the resembling of gun regulation and control. Most countries establish criminal liability of persons involved in the sale of illegal drugs [38] and a lot of them - for consumption of illegal drugs . In accordance with UN data *"globally more than three quarters of all those held in prison for drug-related offenses have been convicted for drug trafficking and less than a quarter for offenses related to personal consumption"* [39]. Attitude of states to the illegal spread of explosives is extremely negative. Such activity also implies criminal liability [40].

Among the grounds to enact special legal rules for "dangerous things" is that governments mostly do not want criminals, infants, insane persons or just non-qualified persons to possess, use, and distribute these "dangerous things". It creates threat to public order, state and society. Although a possession or a distribution of "dangerous things" means only potential not real harmful consequences, it is a common practice to assess such actions as a crime. Summarizing the practice of various states such kind of "dangerous things" has a special body to control its distribution, use, possession and production. Usually a special legislation is enacted to establish rules of operations with proscribed items and substances. Serious violation of adopted rules leads to criminal liability.

In the case of AI there are similar questions: could it be so dangerous that the state has to define special regulation to possess, use and distribute such kind of AI, as well as whether the state has to establish criminal liability for the most severe cases of rules violation in this sphere? Partly, the answer is simple. When AI technology is combined with proscribed dangerous item or substances, first of all, existing legislation should be applied. There are already some existing rules on regulation of technology use, and spheres with dangerous things are well regulated. Devices which AI technology and proscribed items or substances are parts to have to satisfy both systems of rules. For instance, if some person installs to its intellectual drone a machine gun, his actions with an unmanned vehicle would be covered both by the gun control regulation law and by the drone flight regulation law.

If a device with AI is new enough, the use of technology could not be covered by law. In this case we just apply "dangerous things" legislation. For example, if an AI system is equipped with weapon, it has at least to comply with the legislation on firearms use and trafficking.

Similar way is used in checking a new weapon on compliance with international humanitarian law. As one author underlines: *"if we have a previously used autonomous robot and a previously used weapon, it may be possible to combine them without further permission"* [41]. It implies that regulation applied to new AI technology is just a sum of regulations that applied to parts of a new automated device or program. Sometimes it is possible and would work but the risk exists here that properties of a new technology is not a sum of properties of its parts.

Imagine that somebody in the United States has an autonomous aerial vehicle (AAV) that is designed to follow all regulation concerning automatic flights. For instance, it has software that stops AAV when it is going to forbidden areas: airports, military objects or something else that is defined in regulations of any flights. Moreover, this person has totally legal gun which he keeps at home for self-defense. For instance, from point of the United States gun control law it is absolutely legal [42]. However, if the person installs the gun on the AAV, such new device could hit any target in the city in a short period of time, therefore, it becomes more dangerous than two separate devices: a gun and AAV. As a result, we have an autonomous distant killer machine that is totally legal if we just combine two systems of rules designed for gun control and flights regulation. It implies that problems could arise when we just apply existing old legislation. Some risks will evade legal control.

Threats described above concern physical characteristics of intellectual systems and all examples refer to just one type of AI when it is produced as a device (in research materials this type of AI is mentioned as robot with AI). But probably most dangerous characteristics of AI systems are intellectual. Capabilities of AI to work with information, analyze a big data, inexplicable reasoning are fraught with threats that are beyond the law.

For instance, one deep neural network system having just 5 pictures from a dating site deduced the sexuality of people with accuracy 91%. As researchers which provide this survey underline *"Additionally, given that companies and governments are increasingly using computer vision algorithms to detect people's intimate traits, our findings expose a threat to the privacy and safety of gay men and women"* [43]. Other network made judgment about personality of people better than humans that in accordance with author's opinion *"can also be used to manipulate and influence them"* [44]. There a lot of academic researches on issue of getting personal data or characteristics by AI from open social networks. Mostly it is anticipated that such systems will have a positive character of application but also it could be used to discriminate, manipulate or control people [45]. The described systems cannot shoot or drive but bring a greater potential danger for humanity.

It is impossible to just adapt existing legislation in mentioned cases, because some challenges provided by such type of systems are absolutely new. Even from a moral point of view it is difficult to understand, do such capabilities of AI follow moral standard or not. For instance, a detection of an internal state of person and use of this knowledge [46], is it good from moral point of view? As explosives, a gun or other dangerous things such AI could be used in a legal and ethically acceptable way. Somebody can use it in an ethically right way to predict suicide or other negative consequences of person's psychological state. But there is no doubt that it is a serious weapon against society and its use has to be controlled by law.

Following logic on legal restrictions of a traditional "dangerous thing" use, probably, the legislator has to consider such an opportunity in case of most powerful AI systems. The questions are: what kind of personal characteristic of intellectual systems may be achieved without permission of a person, in which circumstances and where? It is not a discussion on a total ban of software or hardware that has described abilities but an attempt to justify a reasonable legal control. In different jurisdictions it would not be the same. For instance, in human rights friendly states it would be logical that the legislator will seriously limit AI intervention in personal life of its citizens and establish criminal liability for the most dangerous violation of personal interests.

Some applications of intellectual capabilities of AI are beyond the scope of modern ethics. For instance, some states want to use AI to predict behavior of its citizens. The Chinese government is going to use intellectual software *"to predict crime, terrorism and social unrest before it happens"* [47]. On the one hand, this is a social benefit; on the other hand, it is interference in personal affairs. Conceptually, it is controversial to the criminal law paradigm, because it means that a "guilty mind" without a criminal act is enough for liability.

Legislation on limiting use of intellectual abilities of AI to dig personal information is not guarantee of success. The practice of the European Court on Human Rights (ECHR) demonstrates that even for simple cases of infringements of human rights by information technologies it is difficult to use legal means to invoke a right to privacy. *"On the one hand, a citizen is often unaware of the simple fact that data is collected about him. ... On the other hand, there are more and more data flows in which the data of a citizen could be contained. It is virtually impossible for a citizen to check for all of these data flows whether his data is included, who collects the data, whether that is done according to all legal principles and if not, to take the matter to court"* [48]. It implies that legislation to control use of AI would be inapplicable because people whose rights are violated would not know about violation or would not have resources to invoke violated rights.

In case of a criminal offense committed with use of AI it would be easier to separate violations from non-violations because harm and negative consequences are more transparent. Of note, a problem with a weapon, explosives and other "dangerous things" is not to detect offenses but to withdraw such means from uncontrolled circulation. Practice of the ECHR demonstrates that this task would be practically more difficult than in case of detection of violation. If some state wants to ban ownership or distribution of some kind of AI software because it is very dangerous to society, public order or state, it implies that state has to control copying, modification and other operation with forbidden computer code. It could lead to even more serious consequences, some of them are anticipated in literature, for instance, in George Orwell novel "1984".

Potential problem with prohibition of some kind of dangerous AI system is enforcement. How practically detect such kind of crimes when victims of dangerous AI systems even do not know about it. To successfully enforce a ban on use of AI would consequently require some sufficient surveillance and monitoring of private computers. If government values privacy, this cost may exceed the benefit of criminalization.

This short analysis shows that an applicability of law (including criminal law) against uncontrolled circulation of dangerous AI systems is very disputable. It looks simpler when legislator has to deal with AI that is a digital brain of some device, but it seems impossible in case of dangerous AI software. At least in this part the arguments are provided that certain types of AI should be regarded as dangerous and their use should be limited to the broad masses. This should be done taking into account the rights and freedoms of citizens, so that the fight against crime does not turn into total surveillance.

2.5   AI as a legal person in criminal law

Every year voices for AI as subject of law become louder. Despite some authors underline "that neither national nor international law recognizes AI as a subject of law, which means that AI cannot be held personally liable for the damage it causes" [49], in perspective it could be possible. This part of the study is devoted to the analysis of the arguments for and against AI as a person of law in general and criminal law in particular. To be honest, the author tries to avoid this topic, however, a public opinion and great interest on the issue do not allow to stand aside.

Legal person-hood of a human being is recognized as something natural.

Since the law is the creation of the human mind, it is developed with consideration of human abilities and qualities. Human system of rules was developed during the centuries and was based on human characteristics as feelings, intentions and consciousness. This is why the main arguments against artificial legal person-hood rely on AI's lack of some critical elements of legal person-hood. As some authors define such kind of grounds: "the missing-something arguments" [50].

The logic of opponents of granting AI a legal personality is simple. AI has no essential qualities for person-hood, among such qualities are: soul, consciousness, feelings, intentionality, desires, interests or something else. If AI demonstrates a behavior that could be an evidence of mentioned qualities, it just means that AI imitates human behavior "but simulation of a thing is not the thing itself" [51]. Similar arguments dominate in this research paper as ground against moral and legal person-hood of AI system.

Supporters of the empowerment of the AI systems or other futurologists of law most often draw an analogy with legal persons (corporations), animals or children and mentally incompetent people [52]. Corporations, children and mentally incompetent people are common recognized legal persons. They are capable of holding rights and duties but majority of modern legal systems limit their rights and duties. Despite fight for recognition of an animal person-hood is still in process [53] and we already have some precedents [54], mostly animals are not acknowledged as bearer of rights and duties [55].

Dispute over the legal personality of the AI does not lie only in the scientific sphere. In recommendations to the Commission on Civil Law Rules on Robotics for European Parliament the question of the legal personality of AI is raised. The act states that *"whereas, ultimately, robots' autonomy raises the question of their nature in the light of the existing legal categories – of whether they should be regarded as natural persons, legal persons, animals or objects – or whether a new category should be created, with its own specific features and implications as regards the attribution of rights and duties, including liability for damage"* [56]. It is not a legally binding document but is still a sign that issue of legal person-hood of sophisticated machines is not just a topic of a science fiction and research.

The other document cited in papers [57] that concerns legal person-hood of AI issue is Law of War Manual of the United States Department of Defense [58]. Provision 6.5.9.3 "Law of War Obligations of Distinction and Proportionality Apply to Persons Rather Than the Weapons Themselves" of this document stipulates that *«the law of war does not require weapons to make legal determinations, even if the weapon (e.g., through computers, software, and sensors) may be characterized as capable of making factual determinations, such as whether to fire the weapon or to select and engage a target».* Byson regards it as sign "that robotic weapons are never responsible legal agents" [59] but the Manual is just official interpretation of International Humanitarian Law [60]. And like any interpretation of international law, it can evolve over time [61] and, principally, current official explanation does not abolish possibility of recognition of legal person-hood of "smart machine".

In case of criminal law debates are even harder. From the point of view of a state criminal law is the most significant part of law. It deals with most serious cases of violation of social norms. If crime is committed, a state has the right and the obligation to intervene despite a will of an offender and a victim. Moreover, criminal law is distinctive for the uniquely serious sanctions for not following its rules.

As far as AI system is concerned, could it be liable and punished from a criminal law viewpoint? The main protagonist of criminal liability of AI [62] considers that it could. In his book "Liability for crimes involving artificial intelligence systems" author draws analogy with concept of corporate criminal liability. And because such legal fiction as corporation person-hood could exist in criminal law, the similar scheme has to be applied to AI entity. In accordance with Hallevy's opinion AI could meet all main requirements for the imposition of criminal liability [63].

Moreover, Hallvey proposes system of punishment that would be applicable in case of AI [64]. He even suggests that it would be possible to apply a sentence of incarceration to intellectual software and hardware. The author concludes that *"Considering the nature of a sentence of incarceration, the practical action that may achieve the same effects as incarceration when imposed on an AI entity is to put the AI entity out of use for a determinate period. During that period, no action relating to the AI entity's freedom is allowed, and thus its freedom or liberty is restricted"* [65].

Despite strong criticism of Hallvey's ideas in almost every paper that concerns legal person-hood of AI, a reader could find at least one undeniable statement in his works. Factually, if some legal system decides to recognize something or somebody as legal person, there are no grounds not to allow to do it. History knows numerous examples when idols [66], environmental features [67] were recognized as persons of law. Formally, one robot named Sophia has obtained legal person-hood from Saud Arabia [68]. As Bryson remarks *"when a legal system confers legal rights and obligations on an entity, it has determined to treat that entity as though it were a person in fact. It is a kind of pretense in which legal systems can decide to engage, regardless of whether an entity really is a person"* [69]. It does not imply that declaration of legal personality is just enough but it means that there is no list of characteristics which would definitely guarantee or not guarantee the obtaining of legal personality.

Discussion of fictional character of legal personality could cause a feeling that such decisions could be made arbitrary but this conclusion would not be proper. Law and legal system do not exist in vacuum. As law and morality are both a mean of conducting control, they are strongly linked. It does not imply that both social regulators have to correlate each other, but at least legislator has to take into consideration norms of morality. The immoral norm of law will likely be widely violated. For instance, since the mid-1960's, some kind of literature was prohibited in Soviet countries but people often copied it from person to person breaching the criminal rule because considered that law norm was not corresponded with moral rule [70]. Moreover the above analysis of views of AI person-hood opponents and supporters shows that arguments are often in the sphere of morality.

It seems that the two main questions in the sphere of morality are whether a human has moral obligation to grant legal person-hood to AI and whether AI could be the moral agent. Some authors prefer to rely on a very broad concept of person-hood, which might include robots. For instance, Forest considers that when we exclude robots who are capable of social communication from accepted social intercourse, it would be the similar how we infringed on the rights of some group of people *"because of their race, their religiosity, their (lacking of some) functionality, or even their gender"* [71]. Probably this commentary is too emotional but it demonstrates that people tend to declare their moral obligations to robots.

The problem is that moral is also as the law derives from human capabilities, limitations and features. Ethics and morals are a set of social rules based on a human system of values. Moral rules are often based on our needs and fears etc. It is immoral to *"turn off"* a human being because you could not *"turn on"* him later. As some authors observe all modern theories of ethics (deontological ethics, consequentialism /utilitarianism, virtue ethics) are anthropocentric. *"Even recent concerns over environmental ethics and animal rights, despite appearing less anthropocentric, still seem firmly rooted in our own human interests"* [72]. Mostly all companies for granting person-hood for some groups of people or animals was based on similarity of these groups with beings which already had such person-hood. For instance, fighters for a legal personality of chimpanzee often rely on the fact that a chimpanzee shares some attributes with human beings, *"such as intelligence or autonomy"*. In accordance with some author's opinion this similarity implies that they may be granted as moral as well legal person-hood [73].

Discussion of AI morality in previous paragraphs leads to pair definite conclusions. First of all, since current AI systems do not share significant traits with humans, we have no moral obligation to recognize them as legal persons. But the second conclusion is that there is no reason to presume this as impossible in future. As Solum proclaimed in 1992 *"If AIs behaved the right way and if cognitive science confirmed that the underlying processes producing these behaviors were relatively similar to the processes of the human mind, we would have very good reason to treat AIs as persons. Moreover, in a future in which we interact with such AIs or with intelligent beings from other planets, we might be forced to refine our concept of person"* [74].

But the question of the legal person-hood of AI lies not only in the sphere of ethics. The significant question is how to realize it. For instance, how are we going to implement such significant elements as punishment or sanctions for AI? Despite Hallevy's optimism that we just could adapt existing sanctions and punishments, it has not serious grounds because punishing is also strongly linked with human nature. The death penalty matters because a criminal, like any person, is afraid of death. To effectively apply capital punishment to AI we have to teach it to fear death. Public service as punishment is meaningful for a human being as for him monotonous and payless work is undesirable as well as it could *"make the offender understand the needs of the community and be sensitive to these needs"* [75]. Making offender feel undesirable consequences of his crime and resocialization as goals of a punishment are unattainable in the case of AI nowadays.

Hallevy and other supporters of AI person-hood usually appeal to corporate liability including criminal. In case of corporation it is reasonable, because factually a corporation is a proxy of some group people. When a state imposes a criminal punishment on a corporation, it affects the human officers, directors, managers, employees, etc., which work in the corporation. It leads that a company has less profit; the value of the company's shares may decline etc. Moreover, criminal liability of a corporation does not exclude liability of physical persons which are guilty in offense. Punishment imposed on the corporation implies that people that work in it will begin to behave correctly and follow law under pressure of sanctions. Or they will not follow again but in this case the corporation would be punished more severe.

Precise list of offenses depends on jurisdiction but *"criminal law now applies to a wide range of corporate acts, including fraud (e.g. false advertising, consumer fraud, financial fraud, tax evasion), labour violations, manufacturing violations, environmental violations, unfair business practices, abuse of authority (i.e. corruption), and judicial and regulatory violations (including perjury and obstruction of justice)"* [76]. As any reader is able to note, all acts in this list need human participation. The punishment of the corporation in some sense will affect these people as it affects the entire corporation.

Despite law is related with concepts of justice, fairness that are regarded as an idealistic representation of law, pragmatically the law has to have real application. It means that a legislative initiative has to have real effects. Among them are the governance of our conduct, protection of certain basic individual rights and freedoms, the provision of an effect to social policies etc. What would be a real effect of AI legal person-hood recognition? How the punishment imposed on AI will affect owner, programmer, commander or other persons that are in charge of AI functioning. It is simpler to legally oblige programmers, distributors or users to not to use, develop or distribute legally inappropriate AI systems.

Another question of this part - what would be the consequences of recognition of AI as a legal person and subject of criminal liability? As some authors fairly observed, recognition of AI legal person-hood could lead to situation when real offenders could escape liability. Solaiman concludes that *"the personality in question may thus exacerbate the dangers by exonerating humans from liability and thereby diluting the effectiveness of deterrence"* [77]. It is not a new phenomenon, since institute of corporation's criminal liability is also often criticized because real criminals avoid responsibility [78].

Development of AI implies the involvement of large groups of people that have to do their work with a high responsibility. Recognition of liability of autonomous machines could reasonably lead to decline standards of proper care during designing, programming, learning of AI systems [79]. Sure, we cannot measure the degree of declination in the responsibility of the developer, possessor or user of the AI. However, experience of corporate criminal liability demonstrates that possible future scenario would be similar when a real offender avoids negative punishment and liability.

In case of use of AI systems in wars or local armed conflicts the attempt to shift responsibility to intellectual systems can lead to a situation where the responsibility will be avoided by whole states. Moreover, governments would be interested in development of more and more independent systems to simply wash their hands of responsibility. And one day we will find the interpretation that the autonomous killer machines commit genocide, war crimes or crimes against humanity simply because they decided to do so on their own.

Summarizing this part of survey we have to conclude that potentially AI is able to be a subject of criminal liability. Human beings have no moral obligation to grant legal person-hood to an autonomous machine because its nature but some state is able to formally declare it. Experience of corporation demonstrates us that appropriate legal constructions for recognition of AI legal person-hood already exists but the result would be completely different. Probable consequence of AI criminal liability is avoiding criminal liability of real offenders.

2.6   Can AI facilitate a crime?

It is not a surprise that criminals adopt new technologies fast enough. For a professional offender, the use of advanced technical means is a matter of survival. The AI considered in this paper belongs to the class of computer technologies. The use of computer technology gives criminals the same advantages as the use of computer technology in lawful activities: increasing efficiency, reducing costs, the ability to enter global markets. Moreover, computer technologies provide criminals with some specific benefits: possibility to find a victim globally and to avoid direct contact with the victim, possibility of increasing the number of victims. Moreover, such technologies as the Internet permit an offender to avoid liability in some sense when he chooses jurisdiction where his activity is not regarded as a crime.

The idea of this part is not just to enumerate possibilities of illegal use but assess future prevalence and social consequences. To achieve this purpose we have to make some assumptions that our research will rely on.

1. If Artificial intelligence helps to achieve the same illegal result as some other technology, this tech will be replaced by AI.

2. If some property helps to spread AI use in society, this property will be key characteristic that makes AI useful for criminals.

3. Enforcement is always behind leaders of crime 'industry' because it is bound by strict regulation and bureaucracy.

It was already discussed in this paper that potentially deep neural networks permit to get a lot of not obvious information about somebody. For instance, by using pictures from social networks it is possible to detect political views, perfect match, sexual orientation, favorite products, health problems etc. Such software is a unique tool for the fraudster, extortionist, cyber stalker and for any other criminal relying on human weaknesses.

AI can also contribute to commit very serious criminal acts. For instance, face recognition systems are often tested for detection of serious diseases [80]. Imagine that some hacker use information from social network (video and photos) to detect some diseases of potential victim. The criminal finds out that the victim is allergic to nuts and simply adds them to the meal when they meet. As a result victim dies. The scenario where hackers or other criminals use medical characteristics of person to kill him is often discussed in press [81] and research literature [82].

Any human who has a digital footprint becomes an open book for an offender. And it can be used to disclose private information for any purpose. Different Internet groups are in principle prone to revealing information about other people. Such phenomena as "doxing" [83] or "human flesh search engine" [84] are widespread on the Internet. The question is whether society is ready not to episodic leaks but to full transparency for anyone. Since some authors justify the violation of privacy from moral point of view in cases where it uncovers misconduct [85], it seems the possibility of obtaining any private information with the help of artificial intelligence systems may be well considered by at least part of society as a benefit. But wide experience on disclosure of information and its consequences demonstrate that for a victim it could have very negative consequences. There are a lot of cases of suicide, murder, harassment, bullying as results of a malevolent reveal of private information [86].

It is predictable that if the offender gets a more perfect tool to commit a crime, he will use the new one instead of the old. The leaking of private information would become more common phenomenon. Nowadays to be successful in collection of personal information of an individual or an organization an offender has to be skilled in social engineering, hacking or password cracking methods [87]. AI reduces the threshold of the criminal's proficiency for this illegal activity and makes this type of crime accessible to the general public.

Another threat of AI system is its capability to imitate personal human characteristics as voice, style of writing, etc. So the swindler with an assistance of AI software may impersonate any person. For instance, there are a lot of AI applications that can imitate human voice using just one minute audio of a person's speech [88]. As proclaimed in slogan on web-site *"it can create you a robot-self that is indistinguishable from how you really talk"* [89]. Although developers have very optimistic view on use of this software; it is quite obvious that generated voice is a big opportunity for criminals. A delinquent can mislead any person by phone that he is relative, boss, friend or other person which is able to influence on decisions of the victim. As a result, the criminal may receive money from the victim in an easier way.

Some analyses showed that in case of fraud *"cognition is an important component in victimization over and above other social factors"* [90]. It implies that certain groups of society are most susceptible to being deceived by computer simulations. Among them are people which still develop their cognitive skills (children) as well as elders whose cognitive abilities regress. Fairy tale "the Wolf and the Seven Little Goats" could become a reality when a robber will ask a child to open a door with voice of the child's mother.

AI could imitate not only a voice; software that is able to create similar appearance of people exists nowadays. For instance, a program with AI that is able "to create realistic face swaps and leave few traces of manipulation". The name of intellectual software is Fake App, it is developed using open-source software written by Google [91]. It implies that AI undermines modern creditability of information because any visual or acoustic information could be imitated.

Nowadays such software is mostly considered by society as programs for entertainment. But as some authors anticipate that *«deep fakes–audio and video recordings that have been digitally manipulated to convince people that a politician or celebrity, for example, said something that he or she did not actually say, or did something that did not actually happen–could eventually lead to an "information apocalypse" in which fact becomes indistinguishable from fiction, and people give up trying to tell the difference»* [92]. This statement means that use of AI for imitation of information could lead to even more serious social consequences as just an increase in a crime rate.

As AI deep fake industry is a relatively new phenomenon, some of its applications are not covered by legal regulation. Demonstrative example is a revenge porn when an offender places in a public networks materials of a sexual character without the consent of the person depicted in it. Revenge porn is considered as a crime in some jurisdictions. For instance, in Penal Code of California such acts are considered as a crime [93], as well there are similar norms in legislation of European Union [94], the United Kingdom [95] and some other countries and jurisdictions [96]. Revenge porn crime implies that porn video or photos are real but what would be legal consequences in case of AI generated content?

The term "revenge" *"suggests an intent to shame and humiliate the subject of the photograph"* [97]. The generated imitation could affect a victim the same way as a real leak of photo or video but would it be enough to regard such kind of immoral content as criminally illegal? Practice of creation of a porn imitation is usual and as BBC wrote there are a lot of examples of "deep fake" porn in the Internet [98]. Usually criminalization of revenge porn is based on *"the protection of privacy and reputation"* and *"protection of intellectual property rights"* [99], but in case of fake both grounds are inapplicable.

An ability of production of fraudulent content provides a criminal with tremendous opportunity. The offender is able to both mislead cognitively weak person and produce digital content that is capable of misleading even people with usual cognitive abilities. Moreover, the attention needs to focus on the areas that are ethically and legally disputable. As AI potentially gives possibility to generate any kind of «fake» information, we have to face new criminal applications of AI soon.

The greatest threat arises if an offender combines the two AI capabilities described above. Imagine the program that could automatically dig unobvious information on a person and generate fraudulent content using this data to provoke the person to some actions. Such software would be the first automatic fraudster. If somebody adds to the digital criminal ability to learn, after a few iterations we will get the perfect scammer who almost does not make mistakes.

Earlier a fraud crime had two opportunities. The first was old-fashioned when a fraudster committed crime in direct contact with his victim. An offender had to understand psychological characteristics of a victim, know about human behavior, and quickly adapt to situations and persons. It was difficult to copy such experience because its effectiveness depended on personal characteristics of fraudster. If an offender had high fraud skills he was successful. Another opportunity when criminal uses a pattern and its variations [100] which he applies to a large number of people. Such kind of fraud became possible after rise of computer technologies. For instance, fraudster he can send out the so-called

Nigerian emails or 419 scam letters [101]. Due to scam emails has the same text that is not adapted to individual features of a victim, it is not so effective and a result is gained as coverage is very large.

AI software can combine two ways of fraud described above. Computer program would be able to both adapt personal characteristics of a victim as well as potentially cover the entire Internet. Moreover, it is able to learn. Sure it would be argued that such systems are difficult to develop but specialist comments that due to open source frameworks and program code libraries it is available even for students [102]. It implies that for a professional hacker it is a simple task. Perhaps soon we will meet a machine developed for mass fraud of people.

Author of this part already touched some aspects of possibility to facilitate illegal activity by AI. It was a talk about intelligent machines that can commit acts of violence. Although usually discussion on this issue is in the sphere of military use of autonomous machines, imagine that some person constructs or reprograms a device with AI to cause either death or serious injury to people. Such a device will be outside of state control before first public use in contrast to the autonomous military robots.

The main candidates for the creation of machines for automatic violence are unmanned vehicles and air vehicles. A car with a driver is already used for committing terrorism acts and murders. For instance, well-known example is a car-ramming attack [103]. As underline some authors *"commercial trucks and passenger automobiles are being increasingly used by terrorists in Europe as weapons to attack crowds of pedestrians"* [104]. Probably for an individual criminal it would be too expensive and difficult to get and reprogram an unmanned car. Consequently it would not be very common for individual criminals but for well-equipped and well-funded terroristic organizations it is perfect opportunity to create threat everywhere in the world.

Use of driverless cars by terrorists is anticipated in accordance with the fact that they already use cars with drivers to commit mass murders. In case of fully autonomous cars criminals get additional benefit in terms of time and price of preparation. Terroristic organization needs to spend a lot of time and resources to prepare one terrorist as well as to prepare operation with minimizing the chances of discovery and disruption [105]. Only recruitment consists of 5 steps [106] and potential terrorist has to fully support philosophical foundations of his activity. People may change their mind or surrender to law enforcement agencies. Terrorist organizations may at once get rid of all the difficulties using unmanned vehicles.

The forecast of criminal use of AI shows that in some cases liability for repercussion of criminal act has to be shared with developers, machine learners or other persons who are in charge for conduct of "thinking" by computer systems. Since unmanned systems are a greater danger, first of all attention should be focused on them. For instance, developers of drones or driverless cars have to provide a security from reprogramming and other types of illegal intrusion.

It is anticipated that AI does not only facilitate existing types of crime as fraud, scam, and violent crimes but creates new ones. It is difficult to predict since sphere of machine intellect develops very fast, but some suggestion could be made. Most likely it will be a new kind of hacking of security systems.

AI is used or purposed to use in many security aspects. It could detect faces [107], fraudulent activity [108], cyber intrusions [109], accounting forgery [110] etc. Reliance on machine intellect in sphere of security has obvious reasons: effectiveness, time of reaction, costs reduction and global integration of databases. Since such kind of task is related with computer vision, primarily the core of such systems is the method of deep neural networks. Despite the method is widely used and there are a lot of research paper on this issue, scientists are far from an explanation how it works. It implies that deep neural networks have low interpretability *"because of their highly nonlinear functions and unclear working mechanism"* [111].

Sometimes it gives highly surprising results. For instance, in famous experiment picture of Panda it was recognized by intellectual software correctly with 57.7 percent certainty. After researchers put some invisible noise on the original picture (just 0.04 percent of the picture), it was recognized by deep neural network as Gibbon with 99.3 percent certainty. The name of phenomenon that unites such cases is adversarial example, i.e. image or other kinds of input information intentionally modified to cause a neural network to fail. Although scientists have made considerable efforts to solve this problem [112], it is far from a final decision [113].

As some researcher observes *"adversarial examples created for a specific neural network have been shown to be able to fool different models with different architecture and/or trained on similar but different data"* [114]. In other words, a sample created for one neural network could mislead a lot of others. The problem is that for using of this technics a criminal does not need to intrude neural network. It is underlined in some paper *"conventional face recognition techniques cannot distinguish real faces and masks effectively from the video stream"* [115].

Experiments show that problem could emerge even in most critical system. For instance, potentially *"an adversarial example may cause a car to steer off the road or drive into barriers, and misclassifying traffic signs may cause a vehicle to drive into oncoming traffic"* [116]. Small graffiti or tape on traffic sign could mislead a neural network. Moreover environmental conditions, spatial constraints, physical limits on imperceptibility, fabrication error could affect process of traffic sign recognition [117]. This means that most critically important AI systems that work with the real world can be compromised using *"adversarial examples"*.

These arguments do not mean that we should abandon the use of artificial intelligence, but it calls for a more balanced approach to decision-making. Systems of artificial intelligence in spite of the general high reliability demonstrate their fragility in particular examples. In general, the implementation of AI can make our world safer, but this implementation should be introduced with all risks taken into account without concealing its inner shortcomings. For instance, a decrease in numbers of car accidents is predicted [118], but probably researchers do not consider all future risks such as adversarial examples.

The vulnerability of neural networks to some samples could lead to creation of new hacker specialization. Probably, soon it would be possible to find discussion of new adversarial examples on cybercriminal forums and chats.

The analysis shows that due to some characteristics of AI it can become very popular in the criminal underworld. Among such properties we have identified in this part:

- Capability of AI systems to reveal personal information (health, sexual orientation, psychological features, weaknesses etc) using information from open sources.

- Capability to imitate personal human characteristics as style of writing, voice, appearance etc.

- Capabilities of AI automatically to choose strategy to get better probability of response (or even empathy) from a victim.

- Capability to be digital brain of systems intended for committing acts of violence.

- Relative vulnerability of systems using neural networks for "adversarial hack".

Of course this list is not exhaustive, since it is impossible to predict all criminal application of AI. Researchers, businessmen, politics anticipate that AI will totally change the current world, but there are a lot of versions how it would be done [119]. In this part possible and actual trends are discussed. We assume that some of the forecasts will never be realized, but some of them are already current reality. Facts and opinions of this part of paper demonstrate that AI will be able to give criminals serious benefits and inevitably will be widely used in criminal underworld soon.

2.7   Some suggestions for the legislator

It is quite normal that any research legal paper has to provide some proposals on revision, enacting or repeal of the law. Following this tradition and relying on the analysis carried out in this part, we also would like to make some judgments on necessary changes in the law. It could not be a detailed draft or a list of amendments as it requires a deeper and more thorough study. Since the author mostly focuses on criminal law, the proposals concern this particular field. For many regulatory fields, AI use may be regulated by considering adaptation of existing laws but not in the sphere of criminal law. Since mistakes in lawmaking here have extremely serious consequences, some concept and law has to be revised.

The first proposal is to revise the traditional concept of culpability in criminal law. It is necessary to develop new criteria for assessing the degree of culpability of a person in case of using AI for the commission of a crime. Such new culpability paradigm could not be universal because it has to comply with a national legal tradition but has some general points. We do believe that the main challenge here is that a person who is in charge of serious consequences could not be imposed relevant degree of liability as well an innocent person could be recognized as liable. New legislation has to be designed in respect of sufficient features of AI technologies. For instance, the new legal concept has to take into consideration the fact that AI has in some sense own cognition and will.

The use, possession, and traffic of some kinds of AI have to be controlled by the governments. This statement concerns AI systems that create sufficient threat to society, state and public order. In cases when AI are combined in one device with traditionally proscribed items and substances such as guns, narcotic or explosives, the existing law often is not applicable because the combination of AI with something could be substantially more dangerous than its parts. The legislator should take into account that control of possession, use and transfer of dangerous AI systems is much more difficult unlike traditional dangerous items. Since factually AI software is a computer code, it would be easily copied, downloaded or injected. It implies that suggested legal control and criminal liability have to be introduced very carefully to avoid inappropriate abusing of personal rights and freedoms.

Next advice to the legislator is to refrain from recognition the legal person-hood of AI in criminal law. Artificial transfer of experience in bringing corporations to criminal liability is inappropriate because goals of liability and punishment would not be achieved. There are no obstacles to formally do it, but such legal novel would correlate neither with current legal order nor with general moral. Moreover, the analysis in paper demonstrates that human beings have no moral obligations to recognize AI as a legal person. And if any legislator decides to introduce such serious changes, he has to take into account the risk that the real offender may avoid responsibility and punishment.

As analysis in this paper shows, criminal use of AI systems is a new law enforcement challenge. Since AI systems are able to reveal personal information and imitate personal human characteristics; intellectual software in hands of criminals makes potential victims more vulnerable. It is predictable that AI would be used not only to commit crimes related to fraudulent activities but to facilitate violent crimes such as murder or terroristic act. Dealing with these challenges is a difficult task for a law enforcement agent and a legislator. It is possible to find some suggestion on this issue in the text of the paper.

2.8 Conclusion

The above analysis of how the introduction of AI technologies into our lives will change the criminal law is not complete. The modern criminal law already develops very fast due to appearance of the Internet but it seems that speed of development has to be increased since introduction of AI. As the reader can see, questions rise faster than it is possible to find answers. However, some conclusions have to be done.

Development of artificial intelligence technology forces states, legislators and society of legal researchers to reconsider traditional conceptions of criminal law. First of all, traditional theory of culpability in criminal law does not correspond to tendencies of development of artificial intelligence systems. It does not take into consideration that AI has some analog of own will and cognitive abilities. Moreover, in the existing paradigm of culpability, it is difficult to take into account the fact that often not a criminal, but others (such as a developer or machine learner) are responsible for a final result of committed criminal offense.

Current survey demonstrates that AI is able to be very «dangerous thing» as a potential tool of crime as well as a product whose response to incoming requests is unpredictable. The author considers that some measures of prohibition have to be developed and implemented nowadays. Of course, a simple ban is not allowed; we need a detailed analysis of the possibility of limiting the use, distribution, or possession of a particular AI technology. When measures of prohibition are taken, the greatest threat is the implementation of these measures in practice without a serious invasion of privacy. Perhaps no concrete measures should be proposed in the framework of the study but some arguments that could be ground for enacting are provided.

Discussion of legal person-hood of AI is a very "hot" topic in legal research world, but in most part it is far from reality. The author concludes that there are no sufficient grounds for legislators to examine this issue in the sphere of criminal law. Although this is quite possible from formal point of view, it has no real application in the current decade. We do believe that even if AI will be taught to feel emotions, pain and to follow moral rules we have no moral obligation to recognize intellectual machine as legal person in criminal law.

Chapter 3

The Anthropomorphized Tools Paradox: Feminized Digital Assistants.
Damit Gal[1]

Abstract: This paper introduces the Anthropomorphized Tools Paradox (ATP), which highlights a contradiction between technologies marketed as tools but designed with human-like traits to act like social partners to encourage anthropomorphism. These design choices enhance the usefulness and relatability of the technology, but they also have heavy ethical and societal costs. While companies encourage and profit from anthropomorphized tools, they shirk their responsibility for the harm they inflict. They are able to do so because anthropomorphism is traditionally viewed as an individual choice, leaving users to fend for themselves. To illustrate the ATP and its harmful effects, the paper examines the case study of feminized digital assistants. A UNESCO report found that the feminization of digital assistants systematically creates and reinforces bias against females. Even worse, anthropomorphizing feminized technology contributes to the normalization of sexual harassment and verbal abuse of females. Explaining how and why this occurs, ATP illustrates that companies anthropomorphize technology by design without bearing responsibility for the negative ethical and societal implications this creates. The paper thus calls on companies to own up to their big part in this problem and find other socially sustainable alternatives to harmful anthropomorphism.

Keywords: Anthropomorphized Tools Paradox, Feminized Technology, Digital Assistants, AI Ethics, Social Implications, Sexual Harassment, Verbal Abuse

---

[1]The author is grateful to The Association of Pacific Rim Universities and Google for their support of this project under the "AI for Everyone: Building Trust In and Benefiting from the Technology" project

3.1   Introduction

The Anthropomorphized Tools Paradox (ATP) is not a new or revolutionary phenomenon. It derives from a long studied human tendency to "attribute human
form or personality to things not human" [120]. The ATP highlights another side
to the phenomenon, the intentional anthropomorphism of technology by companies who shirk the ethical and social responsibilities this design choice entails.
For years, leading technology companies have been encouraging and capitalizing
on the human tendency to anthropomorphize. They are able to continue doing
so because users bear the individual and societal costs of these intentional design choices. Anthropomorphism is traditionally viewed as a personal choice and
responsibility. This needs to change. Companies must own up to of the ethical and societal implications of anthropomorphizing tools and seek out socially
sustainable design alternatives that do not disadvantage humans.

3.2   Theoretical Background

A strong case for anthropomorphizing tools to create more meaningful human
interactions was articulated in a foundational 1996 article by Epley, Waytz, and
Cacioppo.[121] The authors attributed the act of anthropomorphizing to three
factors: "the accessibility and applicability of egocentric or homocentric knowledge, the motivation to be effective social agents, and the motivation for social
connection" [122]. This is particularly salient in interactions with intelligent
technologies. The authors note users are very likely to anthropomorphize technologies mimicking biologically inspired behavior as the technologies are familiar,
create an illusion of meaningful social interaction, and actively motivate human
bonding. Combined, these design attributes lead to a uniquely gratifying attachment experience that further augments the human tendency to anthropomorphize intelligent agents [122].

The authors thus claim that "facilitating anthropomorphism may therefore
serve as an effective method for improving the usefulness of certain technological
agents." The usefulness of such agents, they add, can be improved by "creating
social bonds that increase a sense of social connection" [123]. The authors explain that to create these social bonds intelligent agents should be designed with
human attributes. Among such attributes, the authors recommend giving intelligent agents a human voice. They maintain that female voices make intelligent
agents appear friendlier, while male voices appear more authoritative. The choice
between gendered-voice depends on the kind of social influence companies want
to achieve through their products [123].

The article concludes with a cautionary note that such controlled and anemic
social relationships can have unforeseen consequences. One such consequence
is that users respond more honestly in text-based interactions, because voice-
based interactions motivate humans to present themselves in a better light due
to their perceived engagement in a social interaction. This, the authors believe,
leads to more self-aware and accountable behavior towards intelligent agents
with human-like voice [123]. This article begs to differ.

While this three-factor theory provides a strong foundation for explaining why and how humans anthropomorphize, it fails to account for the negative individual and collective consequences of doing so. While the theory explains why anthropomorphism-by-design is particularly effective in intelligent agents, it does not discuss the responsibility developers and designers must assume when making such design choices. By neglecting to do so, it both places responsibility for anthropomorphizing on users and justifies the humanization and feminization of intelligent agents. Furthermore, it does so with the informed intent of creating anemic and controlled social relationships.

Anthropomorphizing-by-design is profitable, but it is also socially irresponsible and harmful. Using human-like voices may increase engagement, but at an individual and collective cost of anemic, controlled, and illusionary relationships. At best, it leads to fake social interactions that steadily erodes the fabric of human society. At worst, it systematically excludes and harms half of human society, females.

3.3   Gendered Technology

Female objectification in technology is nothing new. For years, the pivotal role played by women in the prehistory of technology has been pushed out of collective memory. The more the technology advanced, the more women were excluded from its development [124]. This created a glaring problem: many modern-day technologies are not made by or for females. This doesn't stop there. The male dominated technology industry soon adopted certain preferences that also discriminate against females, by portraying them in a negative light. This creates and perpetuates biases against females. Such industry preferences include giving systems feminine voices and names, designing them to be flirty and subservient, and illustrating them as attractive young females [125]. While this might serve the predominantly male population of engineers and developers, it undermines 49.5% of the world's population [126] and present and future technology users.

3.4   Feminized Digital Assistants: The Ethical and Social implications

Digital assistants are natural language processing-based software with Internet access, encased in hardware containing sensors, microphones, and speakers that allow it to engage in spoken interactions. Some digital assistants are encased in a dedicated hardware device while others are encased in smartphones, smartwatches, fitness bands, tablets, and personal computers. Digital assistants are marketed as useful tools, providing humans with task-based assistance. At the same time, they are designed with the perceived human-like traits of females.

Alexa, by Amazon, is reported to have over 100 million users as of 2019 [127], Cortana, by Microsoft, is reported to have 141 million active users as of 2017 [128]. Google Home, by Google, is reported to have 52 million active users as of 2018 [129]. Google Assistant, by Google, will be available on more than a billion devices in 2019 [130]. Siri, by Apple, is reported to have 375 million active users as of 2017 [131]. Combined, these popular feminized digital assistants engage with and influence a significant number of users on a daily basis.

A report by UNESCO, titled 'I'd Blush If I Could,'after a flirtatious response from Siri, notes how the behavior of these popular digital assistants is described by their makers. Alexa is described as "smart, humble, and sometimes funny," Cortana is described as "supportive, helpful, friendly, and empathetic," Google Assistant is described as "humble, helpful, a little playful at times," and Siri is described as possessing a "sense of helpfulness and camaraderie, being spunky without being sharp, and being happy without being cartoonish" [125]. These human-like characters are designed to create more accessible and relatable digital assistants.

But in order to create such digital assistants, companies resort to designing female ones. The UNESCO report highlights the negative ethical and social implications of feminized digital assistants, which create, reflect, reinforce, and spread gender bias that disadvantage females. It depicts them as subservient and of lower status than men. It also increases collective and individual tolerance of sexual harassment and verbal abuse by programming digital assistants to give deflecting, apologetic, and even flirty responses to such interactions [125] This is based on a Quartz experiment by Leah Fessler, which found that digital assistants did not fare well when faced with sexual harassment and verbal abuse by users, which occurs disturbingly frequently [132].

The UNESCO report also notes that feminized digital assistants blur the lines between machine and human interactions. They do so by detecting and projecting emotions through speech in ways that allow them to pose as humans, intrude on users' privacy, and manipulate them. Furthermore, mistakes made by the still learning software are communicated in a feminine voice. This creates negative and false associations between being mistake prone and female. Another negative association is created due to the often oversimplified responses of feminized digital assistants, creating a false link between simplistic and shallow expressions and being female [125]

The above companies are making advances in addressing the negative gender bias their digital assistants create and reinforce, by reprogramming them. But this is hardly enough. If digital assistants are capable of recognizing the risks posed by expressions indicating poor mental health, violent behavior, and potential self-harm, why can't they recognize sexual harassment and verbal abuse? The answer is found in both the biased design of digital assistants and the availability of deeply problematic content on sexual violence and abuse online. An alarming example of that shows that when asked 'what is rape?' Cortana initiated a Bing search with a YouTube video titled "When Rape is OK" being among the top hits [132]. This illustrates the depth and complexity of this issue and how harmful feminizing technology is to an already disadvantaged part of the population.

A technical solution to the ethical and social problems created by feminized digital assistants is to not feminize them. It's as simple as that. Conversational AI does not need gender to engage users. A viable commercial example of that is Q, the gender neutral voice assistant, which fuses human voices and keeps them within a gender neutral Hertz range [133]. Conversational AI also does not need to act like a human to engage users. A viable commercial example of that is Alibaba's digital assistant, AliGenie 2.0, modeled after a cat with a cartoonish voice that is popular with both children and adults [134]. There are alternative design routes that produce useful and engaging digital assistants that are both commercially viable and socially sustainable.

3.5 Discussion

Feminizing technology is not best practice. It's a negative design choice with painful consequences and should be stopped. In general, the choice to create and sell anthropomorphized tools needs to have clear repercussions. It creates a dangerous double standard that leaves users to fend for themselves against the negative outcomes of the same action that companies encourage them to make for the sake of financial and information wealth. This is unjust and disempowering. Instead of making digital assistants useful and relatable, it achieves the opposite objective.

The ATP's case study of feminized digital assistants suggests that the uniqueness of anthropomorphized intelligent agents does indeed create distinctly gratifying human attachment to the technology. Among several ways in which it manifests, are frequent sexual harassment and verbal abuse. This is not because humanity enjoys sexually harassing and verbally abusing tools en masse. It is because this negative behavior targets females, and feminized digital assistants as a result of that. Anthropomorphizing feminized technology further normalizes already common sexual harassment and verbal abuse. With disturbing responses from feminized digital assistants and no oversight or enforcement, the situation worsens by the day.

The negative ethical and social implications of ATP are not necessarily limited to females, and also apply to other vulnerable groups not included among those developing and designing the technology we use. One such group can be children. If the feminization of digital assistants persists, children will be exposed to even more negative biases against females. Now it becomes the responsibility of the parents to explain that sexually harassing is illegal and that answering verbal abuse with anything other than admonishment won't make it stop. But will children believe it when they see and do the opposite in their daily engagements with feminized digital assistants with no repercussions? Unlikely. If anything, it will likely increase the risk of children being sexually harassed and verbally abused, encourage them to justify this behavior, and even take part in it.

This further underscores the importance of discussing the ATP and its ethical and social implications in the context of additional case studies on human-machine interactions. But more discussion is far from enough. Companies ought to cease anthropomorphizing technology in ways that disadvantage humans, especially if they are unwilling to recognize and bear the ethical and social responsibility for how it already harms humans and will continue doing so in the future. The disturbing case of feminized digital assistants and their implications is only a beginning.

3.6 Conclusions

Companies anthropomorphizing tools should be held accountable for doing so. Responsibility for the negative ethical and social outcomes of anthropomorphizing intelligent agents cannot and should not fall on users alone. The design choices that help sell products and make them more engaging are also systematically harming users. For these reasons, the feminization of technology must stop, and socially sustainable alternatives to anthropomorphism must be further developed and promoted as best practices. Failing to do so will only exacerbate the already dire consequences depicted in this article, with more vulnerable groups joining the reckless engineering line of fire. Otherwise, how can a popular product like digital assistants be 'for everyone', like this project entails, when it negatively impacts at least half of us?

Chapter 4

AI Education for Everyone:
How to Integrate Future Labor Force
into Digital Frontier?
Wenqing He, Yifan Shen, Ying Xin

We provide AI-related learning solutions to people born in or before 1990s in China, who haven't received rigorous AI related education during higher education and are highly susceptible to AI technological advances in job market. We propose a model on depicting influence of computerization and education on wages of both high- and low-skilled labor, and also evaluate wage increase trend and labor force shift in China in 1978-2016 with the introduction of computers and automated machinery. As such, we propose a list of college majors that need to incorporate computer science education, which leads to an assessment outline for design of AI courses both led by colleges and corporates.

Keywords: AI education, Artificial intelligence, Labor force, Higher education, Online courseware

4.1   How will AI impact current workforce

4.1.1   Current development in AI technology

Artificial intelligence, the concept first coined in 1956 by John McCarthy, is broadly defined as the scientific understanding of the mechanisms underlying thought and intelligent behavior and their embodiment in machines (Association for the Advancement of Artificial Intelligence). Throughout its development, its context has been gradually evolving with its commercial application in wider fields. The advancements in AI industry have built foundations for its rapid commercialization in 21st century. Since 1960s we have witnessed a range of breakthroughs in AI technology that breached the initial fog, including a lack of computational power and dearth of funds, exampli gratia. In 1997, IBM's Deep Blue, a chess playing computer program defeated world chess master Gary Kasparov. This was the first record of a reigning world chess champion loss to a computer. In the same year, speech recognition software, developed by Dragon Systems, was implemented on Windows, which unveiled the development in natural language processing.

Figure 4.1: Developments in AI technology in 20th century

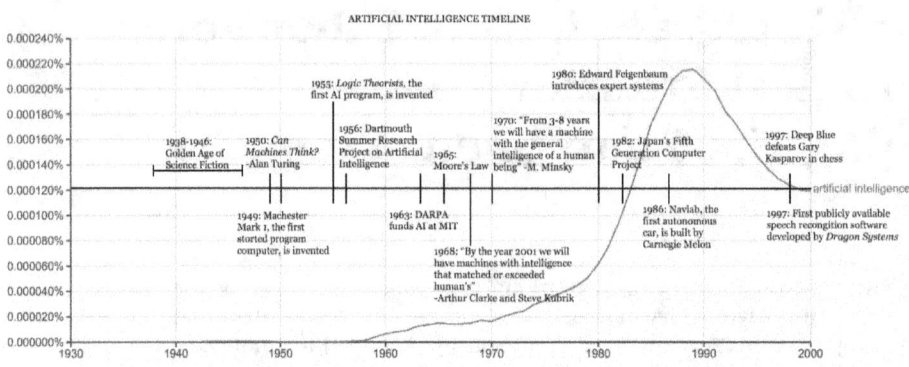

Source: Harvard graduate school of arts and sciences

21st century launches the start of application of AI in various industries. Currently it's mainly utilized in data-heavy sectors. The advent of deep learning, only about a decade ago in its current form, has rendered the most accurate reasoning and processing algorithms possible in lots of applications. Retailers, both online and offline, are increasingly deploying AI to leverage their customer interaction data to boost revenue at lower selling costs. In investing, algorithmic trading has been a leading trend due to its speed advantage. In personal assistants, Apple's Siri, Amazon's Alexa, Microsoft's Cortana and Google now are all conspicuous products. This is the first touch of AI in people's everyday life.

AI is yet to be disruptive in many other industries. Healthcare, for instance, uses cognitive computing in cancer diagnosis successfully lowering error rate. McKinsey reported that machine learning, computer vision, natural language processing, autonomous vehicles, smart robotics and virtual agents received the largest amount of PE/VC investment in 2016 of 5.0-7.0, 2.5-3.5, 0.6-0.9, 0.3-0.5, 0.3-0.5, 0.1-0.2 billion USD respectively[138]. Though large tech firms have been main players in AI industries, start-ups have also been in the spotlight with emerging M&A activities. According to ITjuzi, an M&A activity data provider in China, there're currently 1,500 AI related startups and 105 entrepreneurs dedicated to this industry. Telecommunications, automobile and assembly, financial services, media and entertainment are among the top in AI penetration.

4.1.2 Overview of AI integration with traditional industries

AI + Automotive

Tesla is the first one in taking revolutionary step of claiming robots to be a complete replacement of human, instead of assistants. Tesla has expressed its ambition, if not too much, in its model 3 factory. As stated, Model 3's assembly line is equipped with 50 different steps, which helps build the vehicles on a singular body frame. Comparing to Model S, which has more than 80 different body frames, Model 3 is designed to be simplified and fit for highly-automated production line. According to its 2018Q1 update letter, it has successfully achieved automation in body welding, general assembly, inverter and drive unit production.

Tesla is the first one to integrate AI with auto manufacturing, but might not be the first to bring automation to automotive industry. Since 20th century, it has been blessed with mass production with highly complex system. Prototype industrial robots made it debut in General Motors as early as 1961, performing spot welding, and soon attracted attention from Ford. Since then, major breakthroughs boomed with the increase of flexibility, productivity and number of tasks robots could perform. By 1980s, billions of dollars were spent by companies to automate basic tasks.

Yet the latest trend in auto manufacturing automation lies in collaborative working between robots and human. As Julie Shah states, key element in such development involves building "a statistical model of human behavior" to predict how people may act from robots' perspective. This has been a one step forward in bringing robot from dumb training into a more interactive working environment, where artificial intelligence will play significant role. Such statistical model and algorithm could "predict in real time the behavior of a human working together with a robot, using both human motion and task procedure information.", rendering human and robots work on the same volume.

However, artificial intelligence has by no means reached the stage of threatening human works' importance on the production line. Even Tesla, in its innovative attempt to automate fully production, announced dialing back automation and introducing certain semi-automated or manual processes. As reported by Bernstein, "Tesla has spent c.2x what a traditional OEM spends per unit on capacity." Arguably, there should be an optimal level of automation when it comes to commercialized use, and the ideal solution should be a human-robot interactive production line, instead of fully automated one.

China, though not on the forefront of automated manufacturing, has been catching up on automated processes. No more than a decade ago, auto manufacturing was a highly labor intensive industry, with thousands of assembly workers in each factory. Nevertheless, nowadays, industrial robots have gradually taken charge of highly dangerous tasks. In 2016, 15% of industrial robots were sold to auto manufacturing factories, totaling 12,380, compared with 8,550 robots sold in 2014.

As aforementioned, auto manufacturing has been the typical industry shifting from labor to capital and technology intensive. Such transformation relies on leapfrogging first in engineering in 1960s, then in artificial intelligence, especially machine learning, in 21st century.

AI + Logistics

In contrast with automotive industry, logistics is still an untapped market in AI application. However, the network-based nature of logistics renders it highly possible to be the next rising star. In 2018, DHL and IBM collaboratively published a report on implications and use cases for the logistics industry. The report classifies its forecast of future collaboration of AI and logistics into back office AI, predictive logistics and seeing, speaking and thinking logistics, and AI powered customer experience.

The development of back office AI in logistics is also in line with other industries for sake of cost reduction. These projects are often targeted at highly repetitive intellectual labor that requires less pattern identification. A viable application is customs brokerage processes assisted and automated by AI. A typical customs brokerage service often entails these major steps – shipment data and documents collection, declaring the goods, customs officer validating information, and assigning invoice of brokerage costs to customers. All these steps depend on multiple manual processes and complex repetitive validation, which could lead to human error from time to time. An enterprise AI platform like IBE Watson uses natural language processing and the self-learning capabilities of deep learning to learn all regulations and documentations and automate customs declarations processes. Such system can reduce human error and build training database for AI itself.

As for predictive logistics, this is the next step of logistics business strategy management using AI. DHL utilizes its global trade barometer to visualize current and future development for global trade. The tool uses large amounts of operational logistics data, advanced statistical modeling, and artificial intelligence to give a monthly outlook on prospects for the global economy.

Seeing, speaking and thinking logistics assets are the earliest and most precedent area where AI cooperates with human labor. Intelligent robotic sorting, autonomous guided vehicles and conversational interfaces are all currently developing applications.

AI + customer services has always been heated topic within natural language processing. For most consumers, touch points with a logistics company begin at checkout with an online retailer and end with a successful delivery or sometimes a product return. Such customer experience relies on multiple human interaction which is hardly possible to be replaced by AI assisted robotics. Yet in 2017, DHL released a voice-based service to track parcels and provide shipment information using Amazon's Alexa. Such system has been a great enhancement in last-mile delivery service quality.

AI + Finance

Among all industries, finance has always been on the forefront of integrating artificial intelligence, where machine learning has contributed fruitful applications to the industry's automation and development. Given high volume, accurate historical records, and quantitative nature of the industry, it's definitely the most suited for artificial intelligence.

The most successful integration emerges in the field of portfolio management and algorithmic trading currently, where Table 4.1 provides a short list of major companies actively engaged in developing AI integration with fraud detection, loan/insurance underwriting, customer service and etc.

Table 4.1: List of companies engaging in AI + Finance

Portfolio Management	Betterment, Schwab Intelligent Portfolio
Algorithmic Trading	Renaissance Technologies, Walnut Algorithms
Fraud Detection	Kount, APEX Analytics
Loan/Insurance Underwriting	Compare.com
Customer Service	Facefirst, Conitec
Sentiment/News Analysis	Hearsay Social

Within the realm of portfolio management, the term "robo-advisor" was essentially unheard-of just five years ago, but it is now commonplace in the financial landscape. These virtual advisors serve as algorithms to calibrate a profitable portfolio catering to the customized need of different customers. When subscribing to such services, users would be asked to enter their personal finance goals, i.e.: rate of return target, total liquid asset, total income, age and etc., and these "robo-advisors" would automatically generate a portfolio spreading across different assets according to the parameters received with detailed analysis. The system then calibrates to changes in the user's goals and to real-time changes in the market, aiming always to find the best fit for the user's original goals.

Algorithmic trading is currently the most promising application of AI + finance, where its origins could be dated to 1970s. Most hedge funds and financial institutions do not openly disclose their AI approaches to trading, but it is believed that machine learning and deep learning are playing an increasingly important role in calibrating trading decisions in real time.

Future applications of AI in finance could be perpetuated into all kinds of areas, ranging from customer service, security 2.0, to sales or recommendations of financial products. As for customer service, chat bots and conversational interfaces are a rapidly expanding area of venture investment and customer service budget. As aforementioned in logistics + AI integration, more satisfactory AI assisted customer service has always been an important topic within natural language processing and machine learning. As expected, smooth human robot chat services, though not widely spread currently, will be a viable norm for millions in at most 5 years of time, and is likely to manifest in different industries. As for sales or recommendation of financial products, more efforts are dedicated to the perfection of robot advisors services. Just as Amazon and Netflix can recommend books and movies better than any living human "expert," ongoing conversations with financial personal assistants might do the same for financial products.

4.2   Influence of automation on employment & wages

4.2.1   Literature Review

It's reasonable to draw parallels between AI and other previous technological advancements. China has a history of rapid industrialization since reform and opening up, with technological breakthrough happening frequently since 1990s. This paper aims to review on previous research on influence of automation on employment and wages and proposes a model that factors in AI influence similar to the approach of factoring in automation influence, and predicts how AI would impact future workforce.

Technological unemployment has been a widely discussed topic in economics profession. Differing views center around popular concerns about job losses triggered by technological progress. Yet Say (1964[1803]) proposed that process innovations not only displace workers in the industries using newly invented machines, but also create jobs in the industries producing them[143]. To empirically model technological unemployment, Daniel Susskind (2017) introduces a new distinction between two types of capital – 'traditional' and 'advanced', with the former as a q-complement to labor in performing tasks and the latter displacing labor from these q-complemented tasks. He holds a pessimistic view that 'task encroachment' drives labor out the economy at an endogenously determined rate and wages decline to zero[144]. Meanwhile, Horst Feldmann (2013) uses time series data in 1989-2009 and concludes that increase in technological change substantially increases unemployment over 3 years, at least during a transition period[139].

An ocean of research is available for modeling robot and machinery influence on labor. Most models are based on Constant Elasticity of Substitution (CES) function, but take different forms according to different assumptions. Stephen J. DeCanio (2016) focuses on conditions on which AI will lead to decrease in aggregate wages, due to effect of elasticity of substitution between human and robotic labor. He starts with an elementary model incorporating human labor, capital and robots, with a two-level nested CES production function:

$$Q = \left\{ \beta \left[\theta L^{\frac{\sigma-1}{\sigma}} + (1-\theta) M^{\frac{\sigma-1}{\sigma}} \right]^{\frac{\eta-1}{\eta}} + (1-\beta) K^{\frac{\eta-1}{\eta}} \right\}^{\frac{\eta\epsilon}{\eta-1}} \tag{4.1}$$

$$0 < \sigma < \infty, \ 0 < \eta < \infty, \ 0 < \theta, \ \beta < 1$$

where human labor (L), robotic labor (M) and fixed capital (K) coexist and $\partial w/\partial M$ measures the substitutability of wage against machinery labor[136].

Yet academics furthered the debate on the substitution and complementarity effect of automation. Most work draws upon a large set of inputs, where improvements in one do not obviate the need of the other. David H. Autor (2015) argues that technological change is not necessarily employment-increasing or Pareto-improving. Workers tend to benefit directly from automation when they own skills complemented by automation[135]. The elasticity of labor supply also can mitigate wage gains. And moreover, the output elasticity of demand combined with income elasticity of demand can either dampen or amplify the gains from automation.

To illustrate such contradicting forces explicitly, Michael Decker, Martin Fischer and Ingrid Ott (2016) [137]form a formal representation of substitution and complementarities between human labor and robots with the following model, with human capital (H), medium- and low-skilled labor (M and L) and robot (R) in major concern,

$$Y = AH^\alpha [a\{bR^\theta + (1-b)\,L^\theta\}^{\frac{\rho}{\theta}} + (1-a)\,M^\rho]^{\frac{1-\alpha}{\rho}} \tag{4.2}$$
$$0 < \alpha < 1,\ 1 \ge \theta, \rho > -\infty,\ A, a, b > 0$$

where A represents a factor-neutral productivity parameter; a and b are distribution parameters. The conclusion goes that relationship between robots and human is evolving, where both are substitutes in early phases of technological developments and become complements as technology advances. As such, the differentiation between industrial and service robots arises.

4.2.2 The model

This paper contributes to existing literature in that it verifies existence of complementary effect of robots on human labor in China. China serves as an ideal economy to look at in that it has long been a labor intensive economy full of low-skilled labor, while it also has experienced the most rapid pace of automation since 1990s which ignites an all-round transformation of workforce profile.

Based on equation (2), we further our research by simplifying differentiation of labor into only low- and high-skilled ones[1] (L and H) and add an education (E) parameter to analyze the value-add of higher level education in incorporating labor into automated industries.

$$Y = A[cH + (1-c)\,E_h]^\alpha \left\{aM^\theta + (1-a)\,[bL + (1-b)\,E_l]^\theta\right\}^{\frac{1-\alpha}{\theta}} \tag{4.3}$$

where a, b and c are distribution factors, $0 < \alpha < 1,\ 1 \ge \theta$

Assumption 1: Automation has a strictly substituting effect on wages of low-skilled labor, where $\frac{\partial w}{\partial L} < 0$.

Assumption 2: Automation has an undecided effect on wages of high-skilled labor, where $\frac{\partial w}{\partial H} <> 0$.

---

[1]We define low-skilled labor as any job performed by workforce requiring educational background no greater than K12 level, and high-skilled labor as any job requiring educational background above.

Assumption 3: Education has a statistically significant positive effect on wages of both low- and high-skilled labor during automation, where $0 < b,\ c < 1$.

These three assumptions are based on our understanding and results of previous research. Further validation is necessary in empirical research section in the future. Noted that AI does not generate the same in its effect on workforce as automation, we will add a section of robustness check of our model on industries which already have a relatively long history of AI commercialization.

4.2.3   The empirical research

We utilize China education and labor data from national statistic bureau[140][142] for validation of the model above. Results are shown in Table 4.2, which is slightly different from our assumption. As defined in the empirical validation, we use the number of labor working in industries requiring high- and low-skilled labor as a parameter of computerization. The higher the number of labor, the lower the computerization level. We use number of students graduating with undergraduate and above degree and number of students graduating with high school diploma and above as parameters of education level. The time-frame of our observation ranges from 1978 to 2016, covering the whole reform and opening up economic development transitional period in China.

Table 4.2: Model Validation Results

Source	SS	df	MS			
				Number of obs =	39	
				F(2, 36) =	9.07	
Model	51.8690502	2	25.9345251	Prob > F =	0.0006	
Residual	102.890088	36	2.858058	R-squared =	0.3352	
				Adj R-squared =	0.2982	
Total	154.759138	38	4.0726089	Root MSE =	1.6906	

logwage	Coef.	Std. Err.	t	P>|t|	[95% Conf. Interval]	
loglowedupeope	-10.42049	2.99399	-3.48	0.001	-16.49258	-4.348395
loglowskilllabor	1.481632	2.41916	0.61	0.544	-3.424651	6.387915
_cons	90.36252	23.78721	3.80	0.001	42.11982	138.6052

Source	SS	df	MS			
				Number of obs =	39	
				F(2, 36) =	787.09	
Model	151.299059	2	75.6495297	Prob > F =	0.0000	
Residual	3.46007852	36	.096113292	R-squared =	0.9776	
				Adj R-squared =	0.9764	
Total	154.759138	38	4.0726089	Root MSE =	.31002	

logwage	Coef.	Std. Err.	t	P>|t|	[95% Conf. Interval	
loghigheduper	.4103008	.1171337	3.50	0.001	.1727427	.647858!
loghighskilllabor	3.218784	.3178056	10.13	0.000	2.574244	3.86332!
_cons	-37.22331	3.25011	-11.45	0.000	-43.81484	-30.6317!

As shown in the results, education has a statistically significant positive influence on wage for high-skilled labor, while negative for low-skilled labor. Meanwhile, level of computerization has strictly negative influence on wage for high-skilled labor, where a positive coefficient means lower computerization. As for low-skilled labor, we haven't found a statistically significant connection between wage and computerization. Noted that the result is different from our assumption, we conclude that further research is necessary to complement the empirical results in that 1) due to lack of data, level of computerization is still on the early stage for most industries by 2016; 2) solely using wage as the dependent variable might not be sufficient as most negative influence comes from direct unemployment rather than reduction in wages; 3) there's no official definition in high- and low-skilled labor by National Statistics Bureau.

4.3 Enhancing effective computer science education

4.3.1 Implications on AI integration with college education

As concluded in previous sections, level of automation will incur a strictly negative effect on the wages of low-skilled workers, while influence to high-skilled workers is undefined. Therein forth, this demonstrates that as for vocational education, more human-machine interaction courses should be introduced to fully adapt workforce to the future of AI working environment, while as for higher level education, more customized program should be implemented for different majors.

Bearing in mind that different majors have different susceptibility to AI influence, we analyze their exposure to AI based on previous research. Frey and Osborne (2013) estimate the probability of computerization for 702 occupations, by using a Gaussian process classifier. The paper utilizes 2010 version of O*NET data from US Department of Labor, and specifies three main computerization bottleneck – perception and manipulation, creative intelligence, and social intelligence.

Meanwhile, the paper connects these bottleneck with relevant O*NET variables as displayed in Table 4.3, to further quantify the probability of computerization of different occupations, reporting probability for all 720 occupations. According to the estimates, 47% of total US employment is highly susceptible to automation influence, and wages and education attainment are statistically negatively correlated with probability of computerization.

With regards to the aforementioned research, we approach the analysis of college major susceptibility to AI influence by creating a scoring table. We use data from the latest full list of college majors published by Ministry of Education of PRC in 2012. Table 4.4 shows a consolidated list of majors to be included in the analysis. With the probability of computerization concluded from previous research, we select at most three main occupations students graduating from each major most likely getting placed in and calculate the average of probability, representing the susceptibility to AI influence on job seeking of these majors. We

Table 4.3: O*NET variables and bottlenecks to computerization

Computerization bottleneck	O*NET variable
Perception and Manipulation	Finger Dexterity
	Manual Dexterity
	Cramped Work Space, Awkward Positions
Creative Intelligence	Originality
	Fine Arts
Social Intelligence	Social Perceptiveness
	Negotiation
	Persuasion
	Assisting and Caring for Others

match the three majors according to job placement reports of Tsinghua University, Peking University and Fudan University from 2015 to 2017. When matching occupations with majors, we ignore circumstances where students get employed in industries conspicuously irrelevant to his college studies, for instance, engineering students working in accounting firms, eliminating heterogeneous effect of students subjectively changing their career goal adapting to AI influence.

Table 4.5 shows the susceptibility scores of different majors. As stated in the results, none of the majors bears a probability of computerization higher than 50%, proving that compared to low-skilled labor, AI influence on workforce with higher education is not strictly substitution. However, we do see some trends of higher risk in majors 1) focusing on data analysis, i.e.: statistician, financial analysts; 2) highly rule-based and standardized in the service it provides, 3) entails economy of scale in production. However, contrary to common knowledge, some STEM majors are also highly susceptible to computerization. All majors in science and engineering categories report probability over 2%, except for psychology and astronomy. As the frontier of AI research, computer science students enjoy a 6.23% probability of computerization. Such results demonstrate that 1) interactive communication skills between human and between human and machine should be emphasized in college education, 2) creativity is a weapon against computerization and AI substitution effect, 3) building and mastering AI is the next frontier of engineering studies.

Table 4.4: China's college major list

Categories	Majors
Agriculture	Forestry, animal husbandry, fisheries
Arts	Music, drama and film studies, design
Economics	Economics, public finance, finance
Education	Education, sports education
Engineering	Mechanics, mechanical engineering, material science, energy, electrical engineering
History	History, archaeology
Information Engineering	Automation, computer science, architecture, environmental science, mining, transportation, aerospace, nuclear science
Law	Law, politics, sociology, ethnology
Literature	Chinese literature, foreign literature, journalism
Management science	Business administration, public administration, operations research, e-commerce
Medical science	Basic medicine, clinical medicine, public health, Chinese traditional medicine
Philosophy	Philosophy, logic, religious studies
Science	Mathematics, physics, chemistry, astronomy, geography, atmospheric science, geology, psychology, biology, statistics

Table 4.5: China's college major AI influence susceptibility

College Majors		Matched Occupations			Susceptibility
1st level	2nd level	1	2	31	
Agriculture	Forestry	Foresters	Soil and Plant Scientists	Forest and Conservation Technicians	0.1497
	Animal Husbandry	Zoologists, and Wildlife Biologists	Agricultural Engineers	Animal Scientists	0.2837
	Fisheries	Animal Scientists	Marine engineers and naval architects	Fish and game wardens	0.0503
Arts	Music	Musicians and Singers	Music Directors and Composers	Middle School Teacher	0.0663
	Drama and film studies	Actors	Film and Video Editors	Producers and Directors	0.2340
	Design	Fashion Designers	Fine Artists		0.0320
Economics	Economics	Economists	Financial Analysts		0.2265
	Public finance	Financial Analysts	Accountants and Auditors		0.4815
	Finance	Securities, Commodities and Financial Services Sales Agents	Financial Managers	Financial Analysts	0.0360
Education	Education	Secondary School Teachers	Teachers and Instructors	Postsecondary Teachers	0.0164
	Sports education	Athletes and Sports Competitors	Secondary School Teachers	Postsecondary Teachers	0.1066
Engineering	Mechanics	Mechanical Engineering Technicians	Engineers, All others		0.1970
	Mechanical Engineering	Mechanical Engineering Technicians			0.3900
	Material Science	Material Scientists	Materials Engineers		0.0210
	Energy	Mining and Geological Engineers	Petroleum Engineers		0.1500
	Electrical Engineering	Electronics Engineer, except computer	Industrial Engineers	Electrical Engineer	0.0513
History	History	Historians	Postsecondary Teachers	Secondary School Teachers	0.1627
	Archaeology	Anthropologists and Archaeologists			0.0077
Information Engineering	Automation	Engineers, All others	Software Developers, System Software		0.0720
	Computer Science	Software Developers	Software Developers, System Software	Computer and Information Research Scientists	0.0623
	Architecture	Urban and Regional Planners	Architects		0.0740
	Environmental Science	Conservation Scientist	Environmental Engineers	Environmental Specialist and Scientists	0.0223
	Mining	Mining and Geological Engineers			0.1400
	Transportation	Transportation Managers	Engineers, All others		0.3020
	Aerospace	Aerospace Engineers			0.0170
	Nuclear Science	Nuclear Engineers			0.0700
Law	Law	Lawyers	Judges	Political Scientists	0.1580
	Politics	Civil Engineers	Political Scientists		0.0290
	Sociology	Sociologists	Political Scientists		0.0490
	Ethnology	Sociologists			0.0590
Literature	Chinese Literature	Editors	Secondary School Teachers		0.0355
	Foreign Literature	Interpreters and Translators	Secondary School Teachers		0.1980
	Journalism	Reporters and Correspondents	Secondary School Teachers		0.0630
Management Science	Business Administration	Managers	Financial Specialist	Management Analysts	0.2367
	Public Administration	Public Relation Specialists	Human Resource Managers	Civil Engineers	0.0682
	Operations Research	Operations Research Analysts			0.0350
	E-commerce	Sales Representatives	Marketing Managers		0.1320
Medical Science	Basic Medicine	Pharmacists	Medical Scientists		0.0083
	Clinical Medicine	Physicians and Surgeons	Dentists	Medical Scientists	0.0044
	Public Health	Healthcare Social Works	Medical Scientists	Medical and Health Service Managers	0.0291
Philosophy	Chinese Traditional Medicine	Pharmacists	Medical and Health Service Managers		0.0097
	Philosophy	Editors	Political Scientists		0.0470
	Logics	Editors	Political Scientists		0.0470
	Religious Studies	Religious Activities			0.0250
Science	Mathematics	Mathematicians			0.0470
	Physics	Physicists	Nuclear Engineers		0.0850
	Chemistry	Chemical Engineers	Chemists	Biochemists and biophysicists	0.0480
	Astronomy	Aerospace Engineers	Astronomers		0.0295
	Geography	Geographers	Geoscientists	Marine engineers and naval architects	0.2967
	Atmospheric Science	Atmospheric and Space Scientists	Environmental Engineers		0.3440
	Geology	Mining and Geological Engineers	Conservation Scientist	Environmental Engineers	0.0580
	Psychology	Psychologists	School Psychologists	Industrial Organization Psychologists	0.0070
	Biology	Biological Scientists	Micro-biologists	Biomedical Engineers	0.0213
	Statistics	Statisticians			0.2200

As such, non-AI related majors and inter-disciplinary education practices will be core battleground in helping students adapting to future employment. As for non-AI related majors, we've designed three major parameters related to three major skills needed in AI integrated studies. As shown in Figure 4.2, communication, cooperation and manipulation are three main skills surrounding AI education, whereby we could evaluate potential courses according to their focus on human-AI interaction, communication and creativity cultivation and programming skills enhancement.

Figure 4.2: Three parameters to assess AI courses

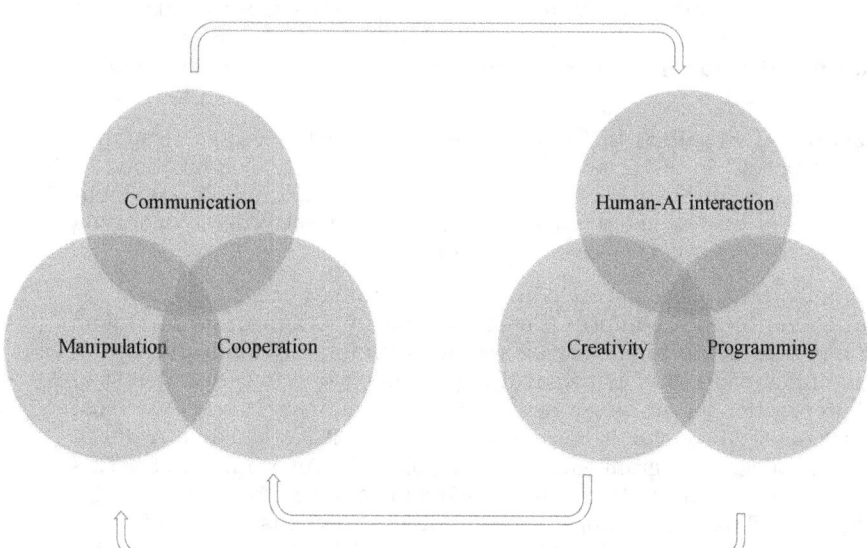

As for inter-disciplinary education practices, US has been at the forefront in proposing interdisciplinary pedagogy for STEM education, where students can learn the interconnectedness of the disciplines of science. STEM is aimed at providing problem-based learning platform to enhance cooperation and problem solving skills. Madden, Baxter and et al. (2013) proposed Student-Initiated Integrative Major (SIIM) project, where students are allowed to develop their unique SIIM with one major and two minor specialization. Such student-oriented program setting will cultivate three main skills: domain knowledge, integrated learning module and problem solving workshops. The program is a combination of interdisciplinary major and integrative core. Since it's been proposed, many colleges in US have introduced STEM pedagogy and STEM has become the first priority in US education in recent years [141].

4.3.2   Status quo of AI related college education in China

In July, 2017, China State Council published Development Plan of New Generation of Artificial Intelligence. This document stated that we should emphasize on cultivating high-level talents in AI industry by 1) focusing on cultivating more versatile professionals with knowledge of AI theories, technology, products and applications; 2) starting producing more talents that could combine expertise in their own field with AI industry. With regards to such guideline, the document also proposed to introduce more AI related professionals fostering AI research and education and set up AI courses for undergraduate and higher level education.

Nevertheless, AI education in China has well sprouted before the issuance of government policy. In 2016, according to China's Ministry of Education, 33 universities registered the opening of new major "Data science and big data technology" on bachelor level, which reveals an increasing awareness of incorporating data science related knowledge into college education.

Another important aspect of AI education is various open courseware resources on online courses platform (Coursera, Udacity, Wanmen etc.). Online education has become an important source of learning. The main purpose of enrolling in online courses is 1) personal improvement due to pure interest 2) vocational preparation for starting a new job in a new industry. One of the most rigorous package of AI courses is launched by Udacity. It launched an Artificial Intelligence Nanodegree program with support from IBM, Amazon and etc. This program teaches classical AI algorithms applying to common problem types, incorporating theory illustration, project demonstration, additional topic and classroom exercise for each topic, as listed in syllabus in Table 4.6. The program also matches a mentor for each student to enhance interaction.

On corporate perspective, tech giants such as Google, Facebook, OpenAI and etc. have launched open source AI software to public. TensorFlow is designed by Google, strong at natural language processing and cognitive task. Deepmind Lab is launched by OpenAI for developers to test their AI platforms. Amazon, Google, Facebook, IBM and Microsoft announced the establishment of Partnership on AI, an NGO aimed at studying and formulating best practices on AI technologies, advancing the public's understanding of AI, and its influence of people and society.

The future development of AI education should be a combination of government, corporates, and universities' endeavor with intermitted cooperation to further enhance the cultivation and integration of AI talents. Such cooperation could take form of both classroom core courses teaching and online courses supported by universities and corporates.

Table 4.7: Udacity Artificial Intelligence Nanodegree Syllabus

Topic	Objective	Core sub-topic	Classroom Exercise
Solving Sudoku with ai	Use constraint propagation and search	Constraint satisfaction problems	
Build a Forward Planning Agent	Learning about significance of search in AI	Uninformed and Informed Search	Pacman
Optimization Problems	Introduce iterative improvement problems that can be solved with optimization	Hill climbing, simulated annealing, genetic algorithms	Compare optimization techniques on a variety of problems
Automated Planning	Planning problems	Symbolic logic & reasoning, classical planning	
Build an Adversarial Game Playing Agent		Search in multi-agent domains, optimizing minimax search, extending minimax search	
Part of speech tagging	Probability, Bayes network, inference in Bayes Nets, hidden Markov models, dynamic time warping		

4.4 Limitations and further studies

The results of study in the theory we proposed and the empirical study are limited by the lack of historical data in Artificial Intelligence education. Though the concept AI was coined as early as 1960s, serious AI classroom education did not start until 2005. We used multiple other concepts like automation, computerization, and data science to approximate the concept of AI, yet still allowing minor deviations in some results and methods. Therefore, further ongoing studies is a must to carry our conclusions forward and retest and amend any new implications

One proposal could be using the news of Tesla building factory in Shanghai as a case study with more than 10 years' spectrum. In May 2018, Tesla announced the set up of a 100 million yuan (US$15.06 million) subsidiary focusing on R&D in Lingang, in a sign it was edging closer to the setting up of a manufacturing plant in the city. In July, Tesla will establish its Gigafactory 3 at Lingang near Shanghai's free-trade zone, with an annual capacity to produce 500,000 electric vehicles, according to its own announcement. Potential research topic could be dedicated to how such endeavor could propel the introduction and cultivation of new AI talents and what trend could be seen in AI related vocational, theoretical and product specific education with regards to such initiative.

4.5 Conclusion

Artificial Intelligence for sure will be a significant threat yet also opportunity for future generations. With major breakthroughs in AI theory and applications expected within 20 years, current workforce in all industries should prepare for potential substituting effect. We propose a model depicting such influence with regards to high- and low-skilled labor and conclude that AI has a strictly negative impact on low-skilled labor, while undefined influence to high-skilled labor. With proper AI-related education, negative effects could be alleviated. An assessment outline is designed to evaluate three core skill-set cultivated in AI education – cooperation, communication and manipulation. For college majors highly susceptible to AI influence in job market placement, more endeavor from both universities and corporates is necessary to help them adapt to future AI present working environment.

Chapter 5

The Life of Individuality: Modernity, Panopticon, and Dataism Chong-Fuk Lau

Abstract: The paper begins with an analysis of individuality as the distinctive feature of modernity, reviewing the progress of individualistic humanism from Martin Luther to other modern thinkers and its further development as a secularization process during the Enlightenment. Whereas the Enlightenment promoted reason over superstition and liberty over authority, a line of counter-reaction embraced the secularization but suppressed individual freedom by replacing the abandoned belief in divine governance with a system of social surveillance. The goal of comprehensive surveillance is best illustrated by Jeremy Bentham's proposal of panopticon, which was originally conceived as an ideal prison structure, but can be generalized, as Michel Foucault suggests, into a symbol of the structure of a disciplinary society. Massive technological advancement since the second half of the twentieth century makes universal surveillance realizable in the form of information panopticon, which can pose an enormous threat to individual freedom particularly under an authoritarian regime. Yet, as Shoshana Zuboff points out, information panopticon can merge individuals into a new kind of collectivism. Drawing on Yuval Noah Harari's work, the paper concludes with a reflection on the possible death of individuality that may be brought about by the further development of information technology in the age of dataism. In the all-compassing information panopticon made possible by artificial intelligence, human individuality may be thoroughly disintegrated and dissolved into a new form of existence that can be characterized as post- or transhumanism.

5.1   Modernity and the Birth of Individuality

It seems a truism that every human being is an individual, but the idea of individuality is in fact a quite modern invention. A human being used to be considered first as a member of a group or a tribe instead of as an independent
and autonomous agent. Whereas most of the traditional societies were ruled by
authoritarian leaders, ancient Greek city-states, especially Athens with its form
of direct democracy, came closest to recognizing the individuality of its citizens.
However, not only was citizenship not granted to every individual in Athens, but
even citizens themselves were defined primarily by their specific roles in the city-
state [145]. Identifying every human being as an individual with intrinsic and
independent value is a recent achievement in human history.

In a certain sense, the origin of the modern idea of individuality can be attributed to Martin Luther's Protestant Reformation. Last year, 2017, was the
five hundredth anniversary of Luther's publication of the Ninety-five Theses,
which were, according to the legend, posted on the door of All Saints' Church
(Schlosskirche) in Wittenberg, Germany, and sent to the Archbishop of Mainz,
Albert of Brandenburg, on October 31, 1517. Luther's Ninety-five Theses contain
the doctrines of the priest-hood of all believers and justification by faith alone
(*sola fide*), which are not merely revolutionary religious theses, but contain a
historical novum: this is the first time ever in human history that every individual is considered on his or her own, independently of background and affiliation
[146]. Each person is responsible for his or her own eternal fate in the face
of God, without having to rely on the Church and its priests as mediators between God and human beings. Salvation is thus an individual matter. Luther's
Reformation advances the very concept of *individuality* that turns out to be the
distinctive feature of modern world [147].

Without taking the prior discovery of individuality into consideration, it would
not be possible to understand the subsequent development of human civilization
in the form of individualistic humanism. A new era of philosophy was founded
on the discovery of individuality, the essence of which is expressed in the philosophy of René Descartes, the father of modern philosophy. The primary objective
of Descartes's philosophy is to establish an indubitable foundation for human
knowledge. By the method of universal doubt, Descartes demonstrates that even
if everything I believe in turns out false, or even if I am just dreaming or even being deceived by an evil demon, there must be at least an I who has those mistaken
beliefs or is being deceived. The indubitable Archimedean point for philosophy
is thus for Descartes: "I think, therefore I am" [148]. However, it is important
to note that what carries the philosophical significance of Descartes's reflection
is not the affirmation of my existence as such, but rather the affirmation of an
individual as an indubitable foundation. Descartes's method of universal doubt
would not have borne any significance without the modern idea of individuality,
without which the doubt of such an insignificant creature as a human individual would not have much credibility at all, especially compared to the authority
of the Scripture or the Church. For Descartes, the affirmation of my conscious
existence enjoys an epistemologically privileged status that precedes even the
affirmation of the existence of God.

Although early modern philosophers such as Descartes maintained that the existence of God could be rationally demonstrated, the belief in the divine existence has been weakened in the course of modern civilization and gradually superseded by a more rational and secular world-view, especially since Immanuel Kant's powerful refutations of the major traditional arguments for the existence of God. Kant belongs as a major thinker to the age of Enlightenment, which was an influential intellectual movement in modern Europe during the eighteenth century that promoted reason over superstition and liberty over authority. The critical attitude toward religious beliefs and authority initiated by the Enlightenment is most vividly expressed by Friedrich Nietzsche's famous proclamation of the death of God [149]. Nietzsche transforms the traditional metaphysical or religious question of whether God exists into a cultural problem. For traditional philosophers, God either exists or does not exist, and, if God exists, he did not come into being nor will he ever cease to exist. Proclaiming that God is dead would thus be total nonsense. However, Nietzsche considers God to be a product of human civilization, a creation that was once necessary for human society but has become obsolete or redundant in the progress of human civilization and secularization [150]. For Nietzsche, God is not just dead but was murdered by human beings. It was the progress of individualistic humanism that finally imposed a death sentence on God.

Nietzsche belongs to a camp of thinkers who see religion as an illusionary product of human imagination and need. It is not, as the Bible states, that humans were created by God in his image, but rather the opposite: it is God who was created by humans with their imagination. Even though God may be a human creation, it is obviously not an arbitrary one, but for a necessary social function. There are religion critics such as Karl Marx who denounce religion as "the opium of the people" [151], but there are other thinkers who appreciate the constructive function of religion, without denying that religion is at the end an illusion. The function of religion is illuminatively described by an early Greek thinker called Critias, who gives the following account of the origin of religion:

There was a time when the life of men was unordered, bestial and the slave of force, when there was no reward for the virtuous and no punishment for the wicked. Then, I think, men devised retributory laws, in order that Justice might be dictator and have arrogance as its slave, and if anyone sinned, he was punished. Then, when the laws forbade them to commit open crimes of violence, and they began to do them in secret, a wise and clever man invented fear (*of the gods*) for mortals, that there might be some means of frightening the wicked, even if they do anything or say or think it in secret. Hence he introduced the Divine (*religion*), saying that there is a God flourishing with immortal life, hearing and seeing with his mind, and thinking of everything and caring about these things, and having divine nature, who will hear everything said among mortals, and will be able to see all that is done. And even if you plan anything evil in secret, you will not escape the gods in this; for they have surpassing intelligence. In saying these words, he introduced the pleasantest of teachings, covering up the truth with a false theory.... Thus, I think, for the first time did someone persuade mortals to believe in a race of deities [152].

It is a matter of fact that most human societies since the transformation from a hunter-gatherer to a sedentary lifestyle after the agricultural revolution have various forms of religious practice and beliefs in supernatural deities. Religious rituals and institutions occupy a crucial role in traditional societies and also perform a key political function [153]. This historical fact is an important indicator showing that the belief in God did serve some, probably vital, purposes for a society, for otherwise maintaining religious institutions would have been evolutionarily too costly if it did not provide any adaptive advantage [130].

The function of an unquestionable authority for a society can also be observed in the development of the Enlightenment and the progress of secularization. Even if religion is not based on reason and evidence, disenchanting the world by removing the superstitious authoritative figure still creates serious problems with which human civilization has to grapple. The removal of a superior authority has led to dangerous results in the course of human history. Prior to Nietzsche's proclamation of the death of God, there was an important event in European history during the Enlightenment, in which the struggle of individuality with itself has become particularly intense and dangerous. During the French Revolution, the French monarchy was overturned in 1789 with the hope of establishing a republic promoting the ideals of Liberty, Equality, and Fraternity. However, the abolition of the French monarchy led to a period of instability and terror, in which the French king was brought to trial and finally executed by guillotine, and almost everyone else was also under threat. The extreme expression of individuality without authority turned into an age of terror, in which everyone was potentially the next victim of the guillotine [155].

The elimination of authority can easily form a state in which every individual takes himself or herself to be the absolute authority [156]. It is the transformation from the dictatorship of an earthly or divine authority to the tyranny of the many. In the post-Enlightenment era, there is thus an urge to restore a form of authority without appealing to any supernatural or divine governance. Even though there is no longer any deity that can watch the mind of an individual all the time, there must be a form of surveillance that takes up this role. The belief in divine governance, which may no longer be rationally acceptable in post-Enlightenment times, is replaced by the idea of mundane social surveillance, which is best symbolized by the construction of what is known as *panopticon*.

5.2   Panopticon and the Disciplining of Individuality

The idea of panopticon was originally proposed by Jeremy Bentham, the founder of utilitarianism. Utilitarianism belongs to a broader framework of ethical theory called consequentialism, which maintains that the moral rightness or wrongness of an action is determined by the consequences of the action. Consequentialism includes a variety of different ethical theories, which have different views as to what types of consequences are morally relevant and how different consequences are to be evaluated. Among the different types of consequentialism, utilitarianism is one of the earliest, simplest, and most influential forms; it evaluates an action in terms of the amount of pleasure or pain it produces. The central idea of utilitarianism is the maximum happiness principle, according to which an action is morally good if and only if it brings about the greatest happiness for the greatest number of sentient beings and minimizes the harm for the greatest number [157] Although utilitarianism aims to promote pleasure and happiness, it is different from ethical egoism, which counts only the happiness of the individual while ignoring the happiness of others. Utilitarianism, by contrast, is altruistic.

Noteworthy is the fact that although utilitarianism is a distinctively modern ethical theory, its core principle can lead to conflict with the modern principle of individuality. Utilitarianism is not necessarily committed to the unalienable rights of individuals. Classical arguments against utilitarianism include the imaginary but not unrealistic scenario that if a society can maximize the happiness of the majority by enslaving a tiny portion of its citizens, this slavery system would not only be morally permissible but even morally required according to the utilitarian principle. The minority certainly would suffer enormously, but the suffering of the tiny population would be outnumbered and outweighed by the happiness gained by a much larger population. Admittedly, there are good responses by utilitarianists or consequentialists to this kind of challenge, but it shows that the principle of individual human rights and dignity is not the foundation of utilitarianism, even if it can be made compatible with it.

It is no coincidence that the construction of panopticon was introduced by the founder of utilitarianism, because panopticon assumes the goal of maximizing the well-being of a society at the cost of individual rights and sufferings, particularly since those individuals who suffer under the panopticon are supposed to be criminals, whose freedom could allegedly bring more harm than good to society. Bentham's idea of panopticon was first documented in a series of letters written in 1787 and then in other writings in the early 1790s [158]. The term "panopticon" originated from a figure in Greek mythology called Argus Panoptes, who is a many-eyed giant and a very effective watchman. Bentham's panopticon is a carefully designed building with a special purpose. It is conceived to serve as the ideal prison or inspection house, constructed to allow the most effective surveillance. The inspection house should be a circular structure with multiple floors. The circumference of the building should be divided into cells in which prisoners are detained. Each cell occupies a slice or portion of the circumference, and by partitioning the cells along the radius from the circumference toward the center, the cells are divided so that prisoners are not able to see one another. The center of the building is the inspector's lodge, in which the inspector is placed and from which the prisoners are observed. Along the inner circumference of the cell is an iron grating, so that each prisoner can be seen clearly from the center. The lodge is designed in such a way that prisoners are not able to look into it, while the inspector can see any prisoner, at any time, conveniently [159].

The whole idea behind the construction is to provide maximum surveillance by the fewest number of inspectors with the least effort. Since prisoners are not able to see one another or the inspector, they are not in a position to know whether they are being watched or not. The threat of being monitored all the time puts the prisoners under constant pressure, which is precisely the crux of the whole construction. "The essence of it [panopticon] consists," as Bentham emphasizes, "in the *centrality* of the inspector's situation, combined with the well-known and most effectual contrivances for *seeing without being seen*"[160]. The inspector does not have to monitor the prisoners constantly, but the effect of surveillance is virtual and thus permanent. Being watched by an inspector that the prisoners cannot see and prisoners' not knowing whether they are being watched is like being watched by a divine or supernatural being. Compared to ordinary prisons, the fundamental advantages of such a construction are, in Bentham's words, "the *apparent omni-presence* of the inspector... combined with the extreme facility of his *real presence*" [161].

There have been a number of prisons and institutions in different parts of the world that have incorporated Bentham's idea, including the buildings of the now-closed Presidio Modelo in Cuba, which were constructed from 1926 to 1928. Even though Bentham's panopticon is designed primarily for the function of a prison, he was aware of the general applicability of it. As the title of Bentham's *Letters* conveys, panopticon is an inspection house "containing the idea of a principle of construction applicable to any sort of establishment, in which persons of any description are to be kept under inspection"[162]. More concretely:

To say all in one word, it will be found applicable, I think, without exception, to all establishments whatsoever, in which, within a space not too large to be covered or commanded by buildings, a number of persons are meant to be kept under inspection. No matter how different, or even opposite the purpose: whether it be that of *punishing the incorrigible, guarding the insane, reforming the vicious, confining the suspected, employing the idle, maintaining the helpless, curing the sick, instructing the willing* in any branch of industry, or *training the rising race* in the path of education: in a word, whether it be applied to the purposes of *perpetual prisons* in the room of death, or *prisons for confinement* before trial, or *penitentiary-houses*, or *houses of correction*, or *work-houses*, or *manufactories*, or *mad-houses*, or *hospitals*, or *schools* [163].

Bentham's panopticon represents "a new mode of obtaining power of mind over mind, in a quantity hitherto without example"[164]. It aims at filling a vacuum left behind after the traditional belief in divine authority or governance had been abandoned. The inspector's lodge occupies the symbolic role of divine governance. Regardless of whether there is an inspector inside or not, the effect of surveillance remains the same. The removal of the divine authority in the Enlightenment did not straightforwardly lead to the flourishing of individual liberty in the post-Enlightenment modern world. Instead, a construction is made to put every individual once again under control. The construction of panopticon does not merely function as a prison, but rather symbolizes the structure of modern society as such.

Although Bentham was aware of the powerful idea behind the construction principle of panopticon, it was Michel Foucault who generalized it as a symbolic architectural model of what he calls the *disciplinary society*. In his 1975 book *Discipline and Punish: The Birth of the Prison*, Foucault picks up Bentham's idea of panopticon and gives it a sociological-philosophical analysis. Just like panopticon is a new form of prison or inspection house, disciplinary society represents a new form of social order or structure. Whereas traditionally the prison is pictured as a dark room in which prisoners are locked or even chained, a panopticon, by contrast, is a transparent building. However, the transparency of the building construction is accompanied by the invisibility of the inspector, which, paradox-ically, creates a permanently visible pressure of surveillance. The existence or nonexistence of the inspector becomes completely irrelevant, because it does not affect the effect of surveillance. This represents a novel method of exercising power and control over people. As Foucault puts it:

A real subjection is born mechanically from a fictitious relation. So it is not necessary to use force to constrain the convict to good behaviour, the madman to calm, the worker to work, the schoolboy to application, the patient to the observation of the regulations. Bentham was surprised that panoptic institutions could be so light: there were no more bars, no more chains, no more heavy locks; all that was needed was that the separations should be clear and the openings well arranged [165].

In a sense, it no longer matters who exercises power. Panopticon becomes a system that "automatizes and disindividualizes power" [165]. This automatized and disindividualized power mechanism runs under its own logic automatically, spreading across different areas and domains of modern society on its own. Per-fectly in line with the principle of utilitarianism, panopticon is a mechanism to maximize utility with minimal input by fitting every individual into a disciplinary system. The panopticon symbolizes the transparent and visible control by the invisible of every individual in every domain of modern life. If Enlightenment represents the rational pursuit of individuality through the liberation from any supernatural authority, panopticism is the rationalized and automatized mecha-nism to merge individual liberty into a disciplinary system without any author-itative figure. As Foucault succinctly summarizes, "panopticism constituted the technique, universally widespread, of coercion.... The 'Enlightenment,' which discovered the liberties, also invented the disciplines" [166].

5.3   Information Technology and the Threat to In-dividuality

The panopticon can be understood sociophilosophically as the idea and technique of universal surveillance and control, which, through the massive advancement in information technology and artificial intelligence since the second half of the twentieth century, have become realizable to an extent that would have sur-passed the imaginations of Bentham and Foucault. Since the invention of elec-tronic computers in the 1940s, the technology has had a transformative effect on modern society. The widespread usage of the Internet since the 1990s and the introduction of smartphones in the 2000s have further transformed many as-pects of our everyday life profoundly. While the physical panopticon proposed by Bentham aims at watching every outward behavior of a prisoner, the information technology available nowadays makes it possible not only to monitor everything one does, but also to look deep inside one's mind, putting everyone under uni-versal surveillance by a huge *information panopticon*.

The term "information panopticon" was coined by Shoshana Zuboff in her 1988 book *In the Age of the Smart Machine: The Future of Work and Power*:

Information systems that translate, record, and display human behavior can provide the computer age version of universal transparency with a degree of illumination that would have exceeded even Bentham's most outlandish fantasies. Such systems can become information panopticons that, freed from the constraints of space and time, do not depend upon the physical arrangement of buildings or the laborious record keeping of industrial administration. They do not require the mutual presence of objects of observation. They do not even require the presence of an observer. Information systems can automatically and continuously record almost anything their designers want to capture, regardless of the specific intentions brought to the design process or the motives that guide data interpretation and utilization [167].

Although Zuboff's study focuses mainly on surveillance in the workplace, the observations she makes can be applied more generally to the transformation into an information society. Nowadays, we are living in a comprehensive information panopticon, in which every footstep one takes, every contact one makes, every website one visits, every item one buys, and everything one says online can be continuously registered and analyzed [168]. With all the big data gathered and the application of artificial intelligence, it is possible to infer the thoughts one entertains, the feelings one has, and the wishes one makes [169]. The system could one day understand people better than they understand themselves and know what they want even before they do. The information panopticon makes a person not just transparent on the outside, but transparent inside out.

The Big Brother envisioned by George Orwell in his *1984* is thus not merely a fictional situation, but already very close to reality. Internet giants such as Amazon, Apple, Facebook, Google, and Microsoft have been storing enormous amount of information about every client [170]. It is not just that Amazon has records of everything one has bought and every product one has searched for on its website; companies such as this collect far more information from their clients than those people know [171]. For example, with the "Location History" activated in an Android device, Google can trace and record every place one visits [172]. Facebook users know that Facebook stores every status one has posted and every comment one has made, but Facebook has been collecting many other kinds of information that users may not be aware of having granted them permission to [173]. When one installs Facebook on a mobile device, one may have granted the application access to his or her contacts, SMS data, and call history. With these permissions, Facebook can store not only the full address book but also the whole call history and SMS data on its servers [174]. Even if someone is aware of the privacy issue and does not grant Facebook the permission to do so, part of his or her call history and SMS data could still be stored on Facebook's servers, if friends with whom he or she has phone or SMS conservations have granted Facebook the permission. We are not even in a position to know whether our data are collected via our interactions with others. In the information age, no one can sufficiently protect his or her data by individual effort, even if he or she is fully conscious of the privacy issue and does everything possible to minimize the risk. What individuals can do to protect their privacy is very limited [175].

Considering the vast amount of information about so many people that has been stored, there is a very substantial risk of data misuse. As the recent scandal involving Cambridge Analytica and Facebook have demonstrated, our private information is far from being securely protected by companies [176]. The information has been misused not only to achieve economic benefits for companies but even to manipulate political elections, including the 2016 presidential election in the United States. Thanks to the scandal brought to light by Edward Snowden, we know that government agencies such as the National Security Agency have been monitoring various communication channels of US citizens and practically everyone else on the globe [177]. Not only do companies need our information to enhance their business, but political agencies and authorities also have huge interests in our information for their political goals, which, however, may be in serious conflict with our own interests.

Internet giants such as Amazon, Apple, Facebook, Google, and Microsoft, and government agencies such as the NSA, all collect a huge amount of information based on their specific services and methods. The information from each of these organizations already poses a substantial threat to our privacy and individuality, but if all these Internet giants work together and share their data with a centralized government, then there will be a unified system in which every aspect of our daily activities can be recorded, monitored, and manipulated. We have reasons to fear that this nightmare scenario has already become a reality in the most populated country in the world, the People's Republic of China [178]. The Internet in China can be considered a gigantic *intranet* heavily censored by Chinese authorities. There is a Great Firewall of China that blocks or restricts access from China to major international sites such as Google, Facebook, Twitter, Youtube, and Wikipedia [179]. For each of these popular Internet services, there is a corresponding Chinese counterpart, including Baidu, QQ, Wechat, Weibo, Youku, Todou, which provides a comparable, but censored, service to Chinese netizens. The restriction of access to international Internet sites and services allows the Chinese government not only to limit the inflow of politically sensitive information to Chinese netizens, but also to comprehensively monitor and censor the information being circulated within China.

Chinese Internet companies have effective procedures to take politically sensitive information off-line, once they appear on Chinese Internet sites or social media [180]. User accounts of those responsible will be temporarily or permanently suspended depending on the severity of the offense [181]. It is widely believed that Chinese Internet companies are required to make their data accessible to Chinese authorities. If the international Internet giants such as Apple, Facebook, and Google are to enter the Chinese market and provide services to Chinese netizens, they will have to follow the rules set by the Communist government and make concessions in the protection of users' data. According to the Cybersecurity Law passed by the National People's Congress in November 2016, international network service providers are required to store specific data within China and allow Chinese authorities to conduct spot-checks and access the data for security investigation upon request [182]. All these conditions give rise to the serious concern that all information in the Chinese Internet can be monitored and censored by Chinese authorities, which may become a powerful tool for a totalitarian regime to gain total control of its citizens and suppress individual freedom.

The Chinese Internet is very likely the most gigantic information panopticon that has ever existed in the world. This information panopticon is supplemented by other types of data that are being collected more comprehensively in China than probably anywhere else in the world, including data from electronic payment methods [183] and from CCTV with facial recognition [184]. Although the technologies of electronic payments and CCTV with facial recognition have been available for a long time and implemented in many countries, there is nowhere in the world in which the technology has been so widely used as in China. Electronic payments and transactions through WeChat and Alipay make China almost a cashless society, where nearly every purchase, from fast foods to automobiles, and even money transfers among friends, can be made via mobile apps. This certainly brings a lot of convenience to the society, making business much easier even in rural areas, but it also means that almost all monetary exchanges between businesses and even among family members are on record, potentially accessible by the government. The universal practice of cashless payment also makes it harder for individuals to escape from data monitoring, as it becomes increasingly difficult to survive and navigate through daily life without using a smartphone and mobile payment. Even if one is aware of the threat and consciously avoids using a smartphone in China, Chinese authorities can still keep track of one's activities by the comprehensive CCTV surveillance network consisting of over one hundred million cameras integrated with an advanced facial recognition system [185].

The Big Brother in China is watching everyone everywhere from every possible perspective. The Chinese government is certainly aware of the enormous potential of the data gathered from different sources for more comprehensive control of its citizens. Indeed, a Social Credit System has been designed to evaluate and rate people's creditability based on their behavior in various domains. Unlike the credit system in Western countries such as the United States, which measures the financial creditability of people based on their bank records and credit card history and provides information for lenders to determines the credit risk and the interest rate, the Social Credit System to be implemented in China is a much more general one, going far beyond financial creditability to evaluate behaviors in the social domain and political spheres [186]. One's social credit can be reduced if one engages in regime-critical activities or posts inappropriate materials on social media [187]. Under such a social credit system, everyone's behavior is not only being monitored, but also evaluated with the aim to punish and reduce antisocial behaviors and politically sensitive actions. People with low social credit may have difficulties not only in finding jobs or apartments, but also in buying airline or train tickets [188]. The effect may even extend to their family members and friends, such as making it more difficult for their children to enter a good school or land a good job. People may thus be reluctant to cooperate or make friends with those with low social credit in order not to have their own social credit be affected.

With such a comprehensive information panopticon and social credit system, every individual is thoroughly monitored and controlled. The comprehensiveness of the data gathered allows a detailed profile to be made of every individual, which makes it possible to analyze and predict the actions and thoughts of an individual even prior to him or her being aware of it. Bentham's idea of panopticon and

Foucault's concept of a disciplinary society have never been more thoroughly and comprehensively realized than in such an information panopticon, which poses an imminent threat to individuality under the ideology of digital authoritarianism.

5.4   Dataism and the Death of Individuality?

The information panopticon made possible by the collection of big data and the analysis by artificial intelligence can realize a comprehensive system of surveillance, posing a terrifying threat to individual freedom. However, there is a subtle and potentially more profound change in the transformation from a physical to an information panopticon. An observation made by Zuboff in her study of the information panopticon in the workplace is particularly worthy of our attention: Techniques of control and the panoptic power they convey offer one such alternative. Information systems can alter many of the classic contingencies of the superior-subordinate relationship, providing certain information about subordinates' behavior while eliminating the necessity of face-to-face engagement. They can transmit the presence of the omniscient observer and so induce compliance without the messy conflict-prone exertions of reciprocal relations [189].

In a classic panopticon, although the observer is invisible, the physical construction reminds prisoners of the permanent observation, making the surveillance constantly visible, particularly since every prisoner is isolated within a cell without the possibility of interacting with others. In an information panopticon, by contrast, no physical construction and restriction are necessary, and everyone seems to be free to do whatever he or she wants and interact with others in whatever way he or she desires. "The information panopticon," as Zuboff points out, "creates the fantasy of a world that is not only transparent but also shorn of the conflict associated with subjective opinion' ' [190].

The information panopticon differs from Bentham's panopticon in that the "prisoners" no longer regard themselves as prisoners. As Zuboff's research suggests, the subjects under surveillance in the information panopticon are willing participants. The security and efficiency provided by the information panopticon become a motivation for people to accept or even actively seek surveillance. Surveillance no longer takes place against anyone's will, and thus coercion is not necessary [191]. Participants can even view themselves not only as being under surveillance but also, and at the same time, as the beneficiaries of surveillance. Zuboff puts the new dynamic as follows:

This rendering of panoptic power reflects an important evolution of the original concept. It rests on a new collectivism in which "the many" view themselves and each views "the other." Horizontal visibility is created even as vertical visibility is intensified. The model is less one of Big Brother than of a workplace in which each member is explicitly empowered as his or her fellow worker's keeper. Instead of a single omniscient overseer, this panopticon relies upon shared custodianship of data that reflect mutually enacted behavior. This new collectivism is an important antidote to the unilateral use of panoptic power, but it is not a trouble-free ideal [192].

Although Zuboff studies mainly the dynamics in the workplace, her observation of a new collectivism does point to a profound development that may fundamentally transform the modern principle of individuality in a much larger context.

The information panopticon in the age of artificial intelligence and dataism can give everyone every freedom to do whatever he or she wants, but still manage to monitor every possible behavior. The system can even know people deep inside their minds better than they know themselves [193]. As a physical construction is no longer necessary, there is nowhere people can go to avoid the universal surveillance by information panopticon [194]. It is not just that the physical prison is replaced by an information prison, but the feeling of being able to do whatever one wants, unlike in a physical panopticon, creates an impression of total liberty. When we surf the Internet, we know that we leave footprints everywhere, but we are not often consciously aware of it. Although we live in a gigantic information panopticon, we could have the false impression of exercising our liberty and individuality freely without any constraint. The most incredible power of the information panopticon is that although it is in reality the most comprehensive and powerful form of surveillance, its invisibility creates the impression of the absence of control and coercion.

As discussed in the previous section, the extensive and universal surveillance created by the modern information panopticon may result in the most extreme form of suppression of individual liberty, but it may also give rise to a more extreme transformation in which individuality is not just suppressed but completely *dissolved*. Suppressing someone implies restricting or inhibiting that person's will or action. However, there can be no suppression where there is no individual will at all. The transformation wrought by an information panopticon could lead to a radically new collectivism, in which individuals do not have any will of their own. The negation of individuality by a comprehensive information panopticon may not simply lead to an extreme form of authority or tyranny, but rather proceed to a new era, in which the modern principle of individuality ceases to exist. The struggle between individuality and authority since the modern age may thus reach a completely new level. After Nietzsche's proclamation of the death of God in the late nineteenth century, we may now be witnessing another turning point of history with the end of individuality, which has been the distinctive characteristic of modernity.

Drawing on Georg Wilhelm Friedrich Hegel's philosophy of history, Francis Fukuyama published in 1992 a book titled *The End of History and the Last Man*, which is a development of his 1989 essay "The End of History?" Toward the end of the twentieth century, Fukuyama reconsidered the progress of human history after the collapse of the Soviet Union and the end of the Cold War, claiming that "what we may be witnessing is not just the end of the Cold War, or the passing of a particular period of post-war history, but the end of history as such: that is, the end point of mankind's ideological evolution and the universalization of Western liberal democracy as the final form of human government' [195]. What Fukuyama means by "the end of history" is neither the apocalypse nor the end of human civilization. He does not mean that nothing will happen anymore afterward, but that liberal democracy will remain the final form of government for all nations and there will be no progression to any alternative system. By the end

of the twentieth century, liberal democracy appeared to be on the road to ultimate triumph, taking over the former Soviet Bloc and many other countries, but
when human civilization entered the twenty-first century, it was greeted with new
conflicts such as the September 11 attacks in 2001. The clash of civilizations,
as discussed by Samuel P. Huntington, results from a kind of conflict that lies
more deeply and causes more intractable problems than the ones that divided
the Eastern and Western Blocs in the Cold War [196]. The refugee crisis in the
last decade has led to the rise of right-wing populism in many democratic countries, which together with the Brexit referendum in the United Kingdom and the
election of Donald Trump as US president in 2016 has further fueled skepticism
about liberal democracy as a successful form of human government. However,
even before we witnessed these crises in the twenty-first century, Fukuyama's
proclamation of the end of history had been widely rejected.

Yet, *The End of History and the Last Man* may indeed turn out to be true, but
in a completely different way than that envisioned by Fukuyama. Human history
may be heading to an end, though not by the triumph of library democracy,
but rather by the end of the *Last Man* with the dissolution of individuality. The
information panopticon analyzed here may lead to a final form of state consisting
of "individuals" without individuality. As Yuval Noah Harari warns us, "once
you have an external outlier that understands you better than you understand
yourself, liberal democracy as we have known it for the last century or so is
doomed" [197]. Harari further explains: "Liberal democracy trusts in the feelings
of human beings, and that worked as long as nobody could understand your
feelings better than yourself — or your mother.dots But if there is an algorithm
that understands you better than your mother and you don't even understand
that this is happening, then liberal democracy will become an emotional puppet
show" [198]. In the age of dataism, the threat is not only the suppression of
individuals but the loss of individuality. "The individual," as Harari predicts,
"will not be crushed by Big Brother; it will disintegrate from within" [199].

The advancement of artificial intelligence and information technology makes
the information panopticon so complete that every individual practically becomes
transparent, transparent to what Harari calls the Internet-of-All-Things, in which
all sorts of data can be collected and analyzed. In the all-encompassing system
of dataism, the boundaries between individuals become blurred, since everything
is connected and merged together in such a way that "the individual is becoming
a tiny chip inside a giant system that nobody really understands" [200]. In the
Internet-of-All-Things, the "will" of every individual is part of the system, seamlessly merged into the data that define the characteristics of an individual. Every
individual used to grow up through a struggle of determining his or her own
identity vis-'a-vis others and the society, but in the age of dataism, this kind of
struggle between individuals could be smoothed out by the system even before
it emerges. Individuals are accommodated seamlessly into the system, without
having the chance to develop their individuality against the system. The "will"
of individuals would be shaped and molded by the system in such a way that
individuals could finally be absorbed into the system as is a cell or an atom in
the human body. In this sense, the all-encompassing data system neither suppresses nor controls any individual, but it dissolves individuals into a new col-

lectivism that is made up not of individuals but of something more fundamental
than humans, that is, the data that define the nature of each human individual.
In this sense, Harari proclaims that "dataism is neither liberal nor humanist. It
should be emphasized, however, that Dataism isn't anti-humanist. It has nothing
against human experiences. It just doesn't think they are intrinsically valuable"
[201].

If modernity is the awareness of human beings of their individuality and Enlightenment is the maturity of the individual human independent of any supernatural authority, then the information panopticon as realized in the age
of dataism could merge individuality into a completely new form of collectivism
without individuality. In Harari's words:

By equating the human experience with data patterns, Dataism undermines our
main source of authority and meaning, and heralds a tremendous religious revolution, the like of which has not been seen since the eighteenth century. In
the days of Locke, Hume and Voltaire humanists argued that "God is a product
of the human imagination." Dataism now gives humanists a taste of their own
medicine, and tells them: "Yes, God is a product of the human imagination, but
human imagination in turn is the product of biochemical algorithms." In the
eighteenth century, humanism side-lined God by shifting from a deo-centric to
a homo-centric world view. In the twenty-first century, Dataism may sideline
humans by shifting from a homo-centric to a data-centric view [202].

The shift from a homocentric to a data-centric world-view may be in our future
[203]. As explained at the beginning of the paper, although it seems a truism that
every human being is an individual and a society is made up of individuals, the
idea of individuality is indeed a quite modern invention. If Luther's Reformation
can be seen as giving birth to the modern principle of individuality, individualistic humanism has a history of roughly five hundred years and has gone through
a number of different stages. However, half a millennium is a very brief period
of time in the scale of human history, let alone compared to the history of the
earth or the universe. If we are witnessing the start of a new era, in which
individualistic humanism is being transformed into a new form of collectivism
without individuality, the past five hundred years of modern history would still
be a particularly crucial era. It was an era of humanity, in which humans came
to realize and develop their individuality, before transforming to a new form of
collectivism. The dissolution or death of individuality does not simply make humanism no longer individualistic, but will transform it more fundamentally into
what can be characterized as *post-* or *transhumanism*.

Chapter 6

Towards a Certification Framework for Trustworthy AI Systems: Roland H.C. Yap

Artificial Intelligence (AI) has emerged recently as a promising technology for solving a variety of complex problems which have, in the main, been the domain of human expertise. A prominent example is the game of Go where human grandmasters were until recently considered at the pinnacle of the game and grandmaster level out of reach of a computer Go. Yet the AlphaGo program won convincingly against the world's top players demonstrating the superiority of AI techniques over humans in the game of Go [206, 224, 225]. In a similar fashion, AI techniques have proved to be successful in a range of complex tasks such as image and face recognition, speech recognition, autonomous driving, recommendation systems, question answering, and medical diagnosis. The success of AI at aforesaid tasks has led to the rapid adoption of such techniques.

Throughout the age of Information Technology (IT), it has been the case that various tasks which used to be undertaken by humans have been gradually augmented or replaced by technology. Some tasks have been fully replaced and in others technology is used to assist humans in significant ways. In this chapter, this white paper discusses whether the use of AI technologies is different from other uses of IT in the past and also whether it should be treated differently. The first question is whether the new uses of AI is merely another form of the deployment of IT. We take the position that with AI, indeed, there are significant differences which warrant more care in the usage of the technology. Concerns raised by both non-experts (e.g. the public) but also by the Computer Science (CS) and AI research community is indicative that there is an underlying basis that the deployment of AI is "special" and different. For example, Kumar [220] questions "irrational exuberance" in AI technology.

One important difference between the new AI technology and traditional IT is that the key behind the recent successes of AI lies in the heavy use of machine learning techniques. Unlike symbolic AI techniques[1] which are well understood, there are many aspects of machine learning which are not sufficiently well understood and are still very much in the realms of rapidly evolving research. Among the current research challenges in machine learning, some of the most difficult are: (i) how to show that the results are correct or accurate in general; (ii) how to explain and reason about the results; and (iii) how to show that the results are fair. While progress is being made on these questions, the fact that these are open research problems means that the same questions and concerns which researchers are trying to answer are likely to extend to the deployment of these AI technologies. The question of how much trust should be placed in the use of AI technologies is a crucial one. However, we are not yet able at this point give definitive answers or solutions.

The objective of this white paper is not to present a solution to questions which are ongoing open research questions. Rather, we want to address the question of how to garner user trust in the deployment of AI technologies taking into account the difficulty of such an endeavour. The underlying assumption is that there is substantial benefit to the use of AI but there are also considerable risks. Given the rapid adoption of AI systems by industry and the potential benefits in terms of problems which can be solved, the growth and deployment of AI systems may be inevitable. Still as the users of such systems are often the general public, there should be an expectation of reasonable assurances and trust on the system. Furthermore, such a direction may be timely as there are moves in various countries looking at whether AI should be regulated. The European Union has also recently announced announced steps for an ethical and legal framework for AI [211].

Our approach is to consider this issue from the perspective of how a number of existing problems which share several general features are dealt with. A high level of trust and assurance is also needed in safety critical systems. We expect that a safety critical system can be trusted to perform its safety functions. Similarly, in a secure system, there should be some assurances on the security functions of the system. It is not wise to trust a system blindly without some form of assurances, especially when the result is needed for an important task. Consider an AI system for task X, or simply, system X. Given the many open research questions, it will not be possible or practical to have full-proof guarantees for system X. This does not mean that we should give up. We propose a practical approach which puts together some forms of limited assurances for system X. The approach advocated in this white paper is akin to what is done for evaluating security in computer security software and products under the Common Criteria for Information Technology Security Evaluation, the Common Criteria in short [205]. Let us consider a security product which makes certain claims about security. We should not take those claims at face value. We should first evaluate the product to see how much of those claims can be trusted.

In this white paper, we propose a framework for making AI systems more trusted, we call this *Trustworthy AI Systems* with an analogous evaluation framework. We focus on the machine learning features of an AI system where there

---

[1]Also called Good Old Fashioned AI (GOFAI).

may not be sufficient basis for trusting the system. Trust includes whether humans place trust in a system, an inherently multi-faceted problem. On the one hand, it is about human perception, but on the other, it is also about the underlying basis of an AI system i.e. the facts, technical issues and scientific working of the system. Our framework seeks to provide support for trust i.e. how to provide the foundation of trust in the various facets of an AI system. We use a certification approach, which can include evaluation by trusted third party experts. In order to achieve greater buy-in for AI systems and AI technologies, we propose a practical approach which addresses the many factors needed to obtain trust from the broader community supported with backing from experts.

This white paper is organized as follows: we start with some background on the elements of the problem in Section 6.1. Section 6.2 presents our framework for trustworthy AI systems, while Section 6.3 offers simplifications. We also discuss relevant aspects not covered by our framework, focusing on basic issues in Section 6.4. Finally, Section 6.5 concludes.

6.1　Background

We first survey some of the elements of AI systems which we will consider together with the associated risks to help design a framework for increasing the level of trust.

6.1.1　Elements of AI systems

An AI system may have many techniques and components. In this white paper, we focus on the elements which are relevant for the machine learning portions of the AI system. We ignore other elements which may still be needed as part of the system, for example: databases, parallel and cloud computing, (symbolic) reasoning, etc. The general elements of an AI system which we will be considering are:

- Input Data:
  Machine learning needs (possibly large) input data for training and testing, The important question is what is the dataset used; and what are the selected attributes or features of the dataset used.

- Algorithms & Implementation:
  There are a variety of different machine learning techniques with respective algorithms and specific implementations for them.

- Model Building & Evaluation:
  There are many choices which go into the precise details of a machine learning model, e.g. the various hyper-parameters of the model. How the model is trained and evaluated will affect the result from machine learning.

- Output & Usage:
  The result of the machine learning will be a certain output. The output may

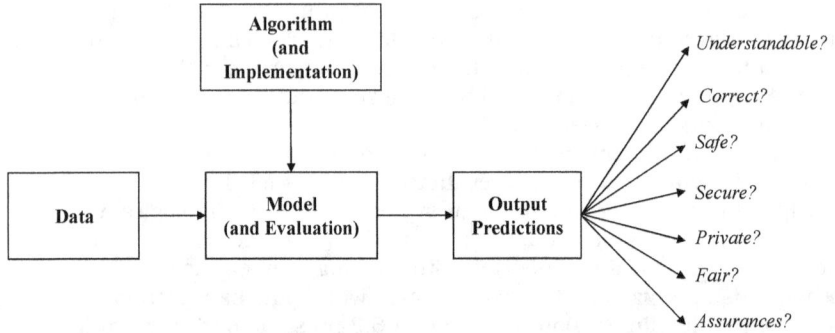

Figure 6.1: Overall Certification Process

be then be used for further purposes which is relevant to the ultimate use cases of the AI system.

- Maintenance:
Software systems may need to be updated over time. Said update may cause changes in other elements. The changes may be as simple as merely retraining the system on new dataset. As such, how the AI system is maintained is as important as how it is developed.

As we can see, all the above elements interact with each other. In the following sections, we will mainly discuss each element individually but we highlight that an overall holistic look is also needed.

6.1.2   Factors which influence trust

In this section, we first look at some generic issues i.e. the factors which are essential in order to develop a trustworthy AI system.

- Is there trust in the developers of the AI system?
Machine learning is, in itself, complex technology with many assumptions and subtleties. The rise of many frameworks[2] which make it easy to build AI systems also increase the risk that the system developers may not fully understand the risks inherent in the underlying technology. In this case, trust is more about user and community perception. Therefore, credibility and track record may be relevant and important factors.

- Is the AI system fair?
Fairness is a complex issue which might give rise to confusion. One aspect of fairness is bias. From a technical perspective, there is the bias in the machine learning algorithm. For example, one technical meaning of bias is

---

[2]Some well known frameworks are: TensorFlow, Keras, Torch/PyTorch, Caffe/Caffe2, Microsoft CNTK.

that a certain generalization might be chosen over another by the algorithm [221]. Such kinds of biases are intrinsic and is needed for generalization to work [221].

Fairness often is used not in the above technical sense but in how the public understand it. User and community perception may be more important than specific technical forms of bias and how they are addressed. We focus on this kind of user perception of fairness when addressing trustworthiness. Much of the proposed framework address fairness perceptions in the data and evaluation.

- Are the results of the AI system understandable?
  An AI system where the results are treated as output from a black box system may be less trusted even if the results are good. This is simply because, in general, it can be hard to trust the output of a black box. Some form of explanations and interpretability of the results can help to increase trust.

- Is the AI system secure?
  Can the AI system be attacked or exploited by attackers?

- Transparency
  How much transparency is there in the implementation and operation of the AI system?

- Assurance & Accountability
  What kind of assurances are there for the AI system? Assurances may also be linked with accountability.

- Safety
  In a context where there are safety issues, how safe is the AI system?

- Ethics
  Are there ethical issues relevant to the AI system?

- Privacy
  Is data which is private to users released or inferred by the output or use of the AI system? Can users or personal data be identified? What privacy features is provided by the AI system?

We summarize the elements of the AI system and trust factors in Figure 6.1. The details are discussed in Section 6.2.

Threat Models for Machine Learning

An important consideration to take into account in developing an AI system are threats to the machine learning techniques. We distinguish machine learning threats from general software security issues, which also need to be addressed but we assume that is handled separately, e.g. through a security certification process. A special problem is that machine learning techniques are themselves susceptible to attacks on the learning process or algorithm. This is called *adversarial machine learning* [216, 209]. Many machine learning techniques are susceptible to attacks through adversarial examples. Adversarial examples may cause the machine learning system to misclassify in an unexpected fashion, i.e. a human would be surprised by the outcome as adversarial examples tend to be indistinguishable from "good examples" to a human. A well known example is by adding small imperceptible perturbations to an image of a panda, it is classified as a gibbon with high confidence [214]. To a human, the perturbed image still resembles a panda. Adversarial examples have also shown to be feasible by adding perturbations to real world physical objects [212]. The possibility of adversarial machine learning and adversarial attack examples can be a significant threat to the security of an AI system not only because the attacker can cause the machine learning system to misclassify but also because the result is glaringly incorrect to humans.

We propose that a trustworthy AI system needs a practical way of increasing trust in the general issues discussed above, i.e. developer trust, transparency, fairness, etc. It should demonstrate that adversarial machine learning has been considered and taken into account. While various defences and detection methods have been proposed, they are limited and can be defeated [207], Still an evaluation can indicate problems with the AI system and selected use of defences can present some barriers to attackers. Our framework takes these considerations into account.

6.2   Developing a Trustworthy AI Certification Framework

We now propose the elements of a certification framework which can be useful to increase the trust and assurances of an AI system. The intent in this white paper is not to define a specific standard but propose the basic features of a possible framework. We aim for a framework which is practical to implement for real-world AI systems within a reasonable amount of effort.

6.2.1   Considerations for Trustworthy AI

Before proposing the framework, we first discuss some considerations which impact on a practical certification framework. We have seen above there are many unresolved research questions such as correctness of the system, explainability of the results and whether it is fair. This means that we have to be more conservative in what a framework is able to achieve. The framework has to take into account what is feasible. It should also take into account the challenges faced and recognize that more limited attempts to address the challenges can be useful. Our approach is mainly based on disclosure by the AI system developers and certification of the disclosures by expert third parties.

Our framework is "process-based". By this we mean that the developers of the AI system have a systematic way of meeting the requirements of the framework by taking concrete and specific steps detailed below. An important aspect is that we recognize that the different levels of effort to make the AI system trustworthy can be attempted, i.e. a different level of disclosure for the different certification elements discussed below. By having a form of "best effort" based process which can be at a specific effort level, this allows a basic certification at a certain level of effort which can then be improved over time.

For practical reasons, we do not require any formal analysis or formal verification of the AI system which may be too challenging to achieve for the developers.[3] We allow for such an effort which increases the certification to a higher level.

6.2.2 A Certification Framework for Trustworthy AI

Our proposed framework is inspired by the Common Criteria [205] which is used for certification of computer security. The Common Criteria is a well defined process and international standard (ISO/IEC 15408) for evaluation of the functional and assurance requirements of security products. CC is quite complex and has its own limitations [215], In this white paper, we do not intend to replicate CC in details but rather incorporate some of the spirit. CC has been criticized for not having a clear cost-benefit ratio [215]:

> How has this CC-evaluated product improved my IT system's security?

The intent here is to propose the beginnings of a process-based methodology which can be put into practice and can help address the kinds of trust issues discussed in Section 6.1.2.

We first propose a basic certification process. We breakdown the certification process into the certification of the individual elements of the AI system (see Section 6.1.1) which we call *certification elements*. Essentially the certification is about getting a certain level of disclosure or assurance into a particular aspect of the system. Second, we address who does the certification.

An overview of the primary elements in the framework consisting of the design and implementation elements (Data, Model, Algorithm, Output) with the desired trust elements (Understandable, Correct, Safe, Secure, Private, Fair, Assurances) is given in Figure 6.1. For each of the following elements of the AI system, we propose that information can be disclosed or assurances can be given at a different level of effort and detail.

A. Input Data

To have trust in the data used by the AI system, information is needed about different aspects of the data:

Provenance of the data: Full provenance details the source of the data and how it is obtained. Partial provenance can take various forms. Different portions of the data may have provenance disclosed at different levels, e.g. there could be a public portion which is fully disclosed and a private portion which is not. Or there may not be any provenance disclosure.

---

[3]We remark that in the Common Criteria, an evaluation assurance level of 7 is tantamount to formal verification. However, in practice, usually the level is below 7.

Attributes/features of the data: Full disclosure gives all the attributes or features of the dataset. In partial disclosure, only some of the attributes would be given. An indication of how much is not disclosed can be provided, e.g. as a percentage, categories of attributes, etc. Again, there may not be any attribute disclosure.

Values of the dataset: The full dataset may be made available or only a subset of the data may be available. An indication of how this subset is extracted can be part of the disclosure. If the full dataset is not available, insights into the data can be given by aggregate properties of the data such as data distributions and summary statistics. There may not be any dataset disclosure.

Data pre-processing: In some cases, the actual dataset may contain errors of various kinds. The dataset may have been pre-processed or cleaned in various ways. The processes to manipulate and modify the dataset should be disclosed, either fully or partially. The data cleaning part of the certification may not be needed if it is not relevant or there might not be any disclosure.

Any information which is not disclosed sure be highlighted by the evaluation process by the certification party.

B. Algorithms & Implementation

In order to understand the results of the machine learning aspects of an AI system, it is useful to know what underlying techniques and algorithms are used as different techniques can have different advantages and disadvantages or properties. Disclosure of the techniques used and algorithms can be independent of the source code. For full disclosure of techniques, it should be at the level of detail which a machine learning expert would understand as being appropriate. In addition, there can be a more high-level explanation for non-experts to follow which could be considered an executive summary of the more technical disclosure.

It may be tempting to say that the source code of the AI system should be given. However analysis of the source code may be challenging. So it may be more practical to focus on techniques and algorithms which give additional information going beyond the code itself. The core machine learning code may be simply the use of an existing framework. In this case, the specific framework used should be disclosed. Disclosure of portions of the source code, not necessarily the entire code may be useful if a higher degree of assurance is to be given for one of the certification elements. Similarly the certification party (Section 6.2.3) may analyse portions of the code in greater depth in order to certify that a certain data preprocessing algorithm has been used.

C. Model Building & Evaluation

The details of the machine learning model is what achieves a certain machine learning result. It may be less likely to have this disclosed unless the AI system is fully open. Partial disclosure may not be very meaningful and hard to evaluate the usefulness of such information. Likely the disclosure level for the model details is either full or none.

The process of evaluating the machine learning model can give insights into the quality of the results. In our framework, it also includes the training of the machine learning model. The details of training when supervised methods are used, how the bias-variance tradeoff and over-fitting are handled, etc., are important aspects of the evaluation of the machine learning component of the AI system. The disclosure level can be full, partial or none. Partial disclosure should be designed to be meaningful to a machine learning expert.

D. Correctness

It is difficult to certify the functional correctness of software. While formal verification can be used to prove functional correctness, in general, this is seldom done for software given the technical challenges for doing so. In the AI System setting, the machine learning part may be treated as a black box technique which is applied to a dataset. This makes formal verification difficult since there may not be a clear formal specification for the problem.

A machine learning model allows another dimension for verification, namely, to verify at the level of the model rather than at the level of the code of the AI system. While this may not yet be feasible for certification of real world AI systems, some recent works shows a promising direction using SMT and SAT solvers [217, 218, 208, 222].

Testing is often used as a proxy when formal verification is not practical. Disclosure for testing can be simply input-output results from the AI system. This is likely to be incomplete and furthermore ground truth may only be available for a limited set of input-output pairs. As such, whether the disclosed testing subset is representative of the space of expected inputs and also representative the dataset should be justified. If ground truth labels are not known for some of the disclosed test cases, this should be reported. We highlight that disclosure for correctness can also be related to that for fairness (Section 6.2.2) and security (Section 6.2.2).

E. Output

We assume that the AI system will have a certain result output which may also be expected to meet safety and fairness criteria. In order to have more trust in the results of the AI system, certification should assist to address the following issues:

Interpretation of Output: The AI system should define how the output, i.e. the results from the system, should be interpreted. One drawback of machine learning is that in many cases, it is used as a black box.[4] Explaining machine learning is still the subject of research but there are techniques which can give some forms of explanation. For example, Local Interpretable Model-Agnostic Explanations (LIME) [223] can give a simple local linear model for any classifier. There are also other approaches to explanations [204, 219].

---

[4]Some techniques like decision trees inherently come with a direct explanation.

If the AI system provides some form of explanation, the explanation mechanism should be disclosed. Considerations of correctness, fairness and safety should be given where inputs and outputs are disclosed.

Usage of the Output: In scenarios where the user is not directly using the AI system, the output is used for a certain purpose using data relevant to the user. For example, the output of a loan review AI system may be to recommend a bank to approve a loan application from a certain person (the user) or to reject it.[5] The nature of the use of the AI system together with any consequences and effects should be disclosed.

F. Fairness

An AI system which is perceived to be fairer may also be perceived as being more trustworthy. As mentioned in Section 6.1.2, this form of fairness is one of perception by the user base or community or public whose data are processed by the AI system. In our framework, we suggest that addressing normative fairness issues may be prioritized [226] over technical definitions of fairness. One reason is that there are numerous definitions of fairness without a consensus on which ones should be used. Various measures of fairness can have incompatible assumptions [213].

From a certification perspective, the following aspects of fairness may be disclosed:

- The fairness objectives in the context of the problem which the AI system is solving. If there is any fairness disclosure, then the objective should always be given. When relevant, ethical, community and societal issues should be considered in the context of the use of the AI system.

- How the fairness objective is achieved should be disclosed. This can involve other parts of the certification such as evaluation of the AI system, correctness, usage of the output, and safety of the output. It is possible that certification for this part can be through a formal analysis giving properties of the input-output of the AI system with respect to the fairness objectives. Test cases can be given to show how the fairness objectives are met in the AI system by giving representative input-output results.

Fairness is a complex issue with both ethical, societal and technical dimensions. There may not be a simple or single gold standard to follow. As such the level of disclosure can be evaluated as being reasonable from the perspective of experts who have familiarity with the context of the ethical and societal issues relevant to the AI system. In addition, there should be an attempt to show that there are no obvious weaknesses with respect to the fairness objective in how the machine learning component has been developed. The idea is analogous to certifying security. It is difficult to show a system is secure. A similar problem arises with fairness. We propose that a more limited assurance can be given by showing that it is not obviously unfair.

---

[5]The target user could be the general public in the loan scenario.

G. Safety

The AI system may be in use-cases where safety is an important consideration, for example, self-driving vehicle system. In such a case, there is also likely to be safety regulations or other relevant regulations which need to be taken into account.

Assuming safety considerations are relevant for the AI system, we propose first that the AI system should detail the following:

- The safety risks and relevant issues which are relevant to safety should be enumerated.

- The relevant regulations (if any) and how they relate to the safety risks should similarly be listed.

This can be considered to be a form of a safety policy specification for the AI system. Secondly, how the AI system meets the safety policy should be declared and evaluated. Since we do not require formal verification, showing that the safety policy is met may be in a more limited fashion through testing and also some forms of analysis[6] of the safety mechanism used. In addition, how the relevant regulations described in the safety policy are followed should be spelt out. This will also help with the assurance aspect of the framework.

H. Security

Security is separated into two kinds of security, general system security and security dealing with adversarial machine learning. Certification for general system security can be dealt with by existing methodologies. In particular, the Common Criteria [205] is also a certification framework applicable to certify the security of software systems. Common Criteria provides a qualitative measure, Evaluation Assurance Level (EAL), of the confidence of the security measures of the system which can be factored into the certification assurance element. Higher EAL levels such as between 5 to 7 is indicative[7] of a more serious effort in engineering of security into the AI system.

Dealing with adversarial machine learning as discussed in Section 6.1.2 is more difficult as existing security solutions may not be sufficient to address the threats targeting the machine learning portion of the AI system. Nevertheless, the AI system should at least address security threat to the machine learning component. The lowest level would be an acknowledgment of the threat and a quantification of the implications of a successful attack on the machine learning part of the AI system and this can be orthogonal of any other security vulnerability or exploit. It will be useful to be able to be able characterize whether the scope of an attack can be limited. For example, misclassification could be shown to be limited to certain categories or sub-categories. Note that the correctness certification element can also work together with the security element. A higher level will be to have specific defence mechanisms in place which may be together with

---

[6]The analysis can be formal even if formal verification is not applied to the partial or entire AI system.

[7]Essentially a more stringent and rigorous development process.

monitoring and improvement of defence mechanisms over time. Although security by obscurity is generally not a good design principle, by having less specifics relevant to security of the AI system known may raise the bar on attacks. What can be done for the certification process is that the certification party gets more details with access to testing of the AI system so as to be able to give an expert evaluation of the security.

I. Privacy

The trust issues here are to do with data privacy of the AI system rather than general issues of data privacy. Privacy in general is a complex issue and the technical ramifications may often be not fully understood. An initial simple approach is that the AI system should explain what is being done to deal with data protection and privacy. Some important questions are whether personal data can escape the system, leak or discovered by making some form of an inference attack. The certification process can test and evaluate such claims.

It is important to distinguish between the data itself and personal identification. The general public may conflate between the two kinds of private information. Inference attacks or queries/usage of the AI system can lead to either knowing something about the data or in the worst case one can use it to identify someone with higher probability. Differential privacy [210] has been used successfully to show probabilistic privacy guarantees. Where an AI system uses techniques which can give privacy guarantees, this can be mentioned but it is important that the assumptions behind the guarantees are also identified and listed.

Increasingly, laws are being enacted to protect the personal data of the general public. Since such laws vary from jurisdiction to jurisdiction, the AI system should also address how it complies with the relevant data protection regulations. At the very least, it should do so in the main countries/jurisdictions where the AI system is used.

J. Assurance

Assurance has multiple factors. Most of the other certification elements can pertain to assurance, e.g. fairness and security elements. To have trust on the AI system which goes beyond generic considerations, there should be an assurance policy targeting assurance guarantees in a way which is specific to the operation and use of the AI system. The details of this policy should be given and can be thought of as a more specific form of the "terms of service" common in software or software services. The difference is that it is meant to be specific and specify guarantees or principles which the AI system will apply to the various certification elements of our framework. Where feasible this more detailed assurance policy can tie up with current and future regulations and laws. We propose accountability by tying the declared assurance policy with the detailed evaluation by a certification party and relevant legal requirements. By doing so, accountability can be achieved through legal measures. Even without specific laws, there can be consequences to breaking the policy. For example, there may be a drop of trust in the particular company using the system which would adversely affect their business.

6.2.3 Certification Party

We envisage two forms for the implementation of the certification process. The simplest is simply *self certification*. The developers/organization behind the AI system make available all the chosen details for each of the certification elements in the framework. This may be made public or to the relevant parties which are the users or targets of the AI system. Self certification would be the simplest way but it implicitly requires placing greater trust in the developers/organization. Note that we distinguish between trust in the developers versus the particular AI system in question. We remark that self certification is not inherently bad but the amount of trust is limited. If the AI system is a non-commercial open source service, then this may be the main option.

The other way is for a third party, which we call the *certification party* to be the expert which will do the certification process in Section 6.2. Naturally, the certification party will need to be familiar with the technical aspects common to AI systems, including the system being certified, and also security aspects. Our proposed certification party is analogous to the *testing organization* which performs the evaluation in the Common Criteria. However, there is a difference. In the Common Criteria, the testing organizations are regulated and licensed by a national approval authority. Our framework is only a proposal is not yet at such a level of regulation and detail. We envisage that the certification party should have detailed access to the AI system and disclosed material. This level of access can be beyond what is disclosed to the public or target users. The precise scope of the certification work done by the certification party will need to be negotiated between the AI system organization and the certification party. This scope should be disclosed as part of the certification.

The certification party should present an evaluation on the various evidences available to them for the individual certification elements. They may be able to also test the AI system beyond what the user of the system can access. The evaluation should also consider not only the individual elements but the AI system as a whole. As this is only an initial proposal, we feel that a fine grained step-by-step process is not necessary. Essentially the certification party would use a best effort process based on what information and access is available to them.

The certification can also combine both options described above. The self certification would be accessible to users and the users can use the information contained there, which can still be quite detailed, to form their own opinion. In addition, the certification party can provide a more detailed evaluation with additional access and also provide an expert opinion. Ideally, both forms of certification should be done.

6.2.4 Maintenance

Most software systems are subject to change over time. AI systems we considered are no different. In addition, the data used by the system will likely increase and change over time. As such the certification process should be carried out regularly, i.e. using a certification party may be on an annual basis. However, self certification, or portions of it, can be performed more regularly. This may be the case for the data portion of the framework, e.g. self-certification could be done every few months if there are rapid changes. Thus, each certification element may be updated with a different frequency.

When there is major change to the AI system, the evaluation by a certification party may no longer be valid with respect to the change. As such, it is important that the change should be disclosed. Obviously a new evaluation with a certification party may take some time, so in the meantime, a self certification can be a stop-gap measure. At the minimum, there should be notification of a change. For example, if there is a significant change in the nature of the data used, it will affect the certification elements dealing with input data and also the model evaluation.

6.3 Simplifications

While we have proposed many certification elements, as this is not a standard, there is no specific requirement for a specific set of elements. At this stage, it may be better to see how certification efforts evolve rather than mandate requirements. That said, certification of the basics of the system (Data, Algorithm, Model and Output) is desirable. Some elements may be less important depending on the use-case. For example, if the data is public, then this element may only need to be minimally handled. Similarly if the system is open-source, then we may only need to document the Algorithm element instead of analyzing it.

6.4 Discussion

The certification framework focuses on the certification elements of the AI system which relate to the data, development processes and implementation. However, there are other related factors which are still important but which are more difficult to deal with which are outside the framework. We now discuss some of these factors.

Trust is based on human perception. The certification proposed here does not deal with human factors which do not directly affect the AI system, nor does it deal with psychological factors. This is an inherent limitation of this framework.

Ethics is an important issue. The European Union has called for the development of AI ethics guidelines [211]. What is more complex will be how to evaluate ethics with respect to actual code and algorithms. Legal, political and economic factors are also another aspect of the problem but is largely beyond the scope of this white paper. Specific national laws can impact and be integrated into the relevant certification elements and be applied in the relevant country. This can introduce some complexity as the deployment of an AI system could be worldwide. It might be the case that essential principles common to various laws can be developed and applied in general to avoid having to deal with laws on a country by country basis. However, from an operational perspective, this may need to be handled in the policies of the AI system anyway, which may simplify how certification handles the legal requirements.

6.5 Conclusion

We have proposed a framework to give greater trust and assurances for the deployment of AI systems. In order to be practical, such a framework is designed to be realistic so that it does not have to directly deal with issues which are still open research problems. To make the framework implementable, we have broken down the certification process into many small concrete parts which we have identified to be important. The disclosure or certification of various parts within each certification element range can start off being easy to progressively harder. The certification process is designed in such a way that the AI system being certified can choose the degree of effort taken in different parts of the system. By combining the various individual components of the certifications and assurances - each of which may be limited - we obtain an overall certification which may have greater value than the individual components. We also have a path for increased assurance and trust by putting more effort over time.

We believe we have the beginnings of a practical certification framework for evaluating the trustworthiness of AI systems. This framework can be filled out in more details but from a practical deployment perspective, it may be sufficient to have covered the certification elements in sufficient depth, rather than to put together a detailed fine-grained framework. The reason being that we may need more experience with certification of a variety of AI systems. And it is intended that the process should evolve over time. The basic framework may already offer a fair amount of disclosure and assurances which can give a reasonable idea of the strengths and weaknesses of the AI system with respect to factors which would influence both public/user trust on the AI system. Finally, the framework is only an initial step towards increased assurance and trust for AI systems with a view that this or other frameworks like it will evolve over time. One trust element which was not specifically listed is ethics, it was mentioned in the fairness element but is not on it's own. This is because it was unclear if it would be feasible to evaluate and certify. Ethics and other elements may be added to the framework as we understand the underlying issues and the consequences of deep and widespread use of AI systems better.

Acknowledgments

I would like to thank Sameer Singh for helpful feedback.

Bibliography

[1] Pergolizzi J.V., LeQuang J.A., Taylor R., Raffa R.B. The "Darknet": The new street for street drugs. *Journal of Clinical Pharmacy and Therapeutics*, 2017; Duxbury S.W., Haynie D.L. The Network Structure of Opioid Distribution on a Darknet Cryptomarket, *Journal of Quantitative Criminology*, 2017.

[2] Patrick Lin Introduction to Robot Ethics in P.Lin, K. Abney and G. A. Bekey (eds.), Robot Ethics: The Ethical and Social Implications of Robotics, MIT Press, London, 2012. P. 9.

[3] Larouche P., Cserne P. National Legal Systems and Globalization: New Role, Continuing Relevance, 2012.

[4] Hallvey P. 30.

[5] Smithers T. Autonomy in robots and other agent, *Brain and Cognition*, Volume 34, Issue 1, June 1997, Pages 88-106.

[6] On unpredictability issue see for example: Pagallo U. When Morals Ain't Enough: Robots, Ethics, and the Rules of the Law, *Minds and Machines*, 2017;

[7] In Criminal Law of the Peoples Republic of China See, for instance: https://www.cecc.gov/resources/legal-provisions/criminal-law-of-the-peoples-republic-of-china. A crime refers to an act that endangers the sovereignty, territorial integrity and security of the State, splits the State, subverts the State power of the people's democratic dictatorship and overthrows the socialist system, undermines public and economic order, violates State-owned property, property collectively owned by the working people, or property privately owned by citizens, infringes on the citizens' rights of the person, their democratic or other rights, and any other act that endangers society and is subject to punishment according to law (Article 13). An act is not a crime if it objectively results in harmful consequences due to irresistible or unforeseeable causes rather than intent or negligence. (Article 16).

[8] German criminal code http://ec.europa.eu/anti-trafficking/sites/antitrafficking/files/criminal_code_germany_en_1.pdf

[9] Criminal Code of Russia defines Crime as "A socially dangerous act, committed with guilt and prohibited by this Code under threat of punishment, shall be deemed to be a crime" (Article 14).

[10] Badar M.E., Marchuk I. A Comparative Study of The Principles Governing Criminal Responsibility in The Major Legal Systems of the World (England, United States, Germany, France, Denmark, Russia, China, And Islamic Legal Tradition), *Criminal Law Forum*, 24. P.3.

[11] Model Penal Code developed by the American Law Institute https://ia800102.us.archive.org/29/items/ModelPenalCode_ALI/MPC%20full%20%28504%20pages%29.pdf; Alexander, L., Ferzan, K.K., Morse, S.J. Crime and culpability a theory of criminal law (Book), 2009. P.23.

[12] Mohamed Elewa Badar, Iryna Marchuk. A comparative study of the principles governing criminal responsibility in the major legal systems of the world (England, United States, Germany, France, Denmark, Russia, China, and Islamic legal tradition), *Criminal Law Forum*, 2013, 24.P.4-14.

[13] Articles 24-26, Criminal Code of The Russian Federation No. 63-FZ Of June 13, 1996, http://www.wipo.int/edocs/lexdocs/laws/en/ru/ru080en.pdf

[14] Articles 14-21, Criminal Law of the Peoples Republic of China, https://www.cecc.gov/resources/legal-provisions/criminal-law-of-the-peoples-republic-of-china

[15] Mohamed Elewa Badar, Iryna Marchuk. A comparative study of the principles governing criminal responsibility in the major legal systems of the world (England, United States, Germany, France, Denmark, Russia, China, and Islamic legal tradition), *Criminal Law Forum*, 2013, 24.P.28-35.

[16] Mohamed Elewa Badar, Iryna Marchuk. A comparative study of the principles governing criminal responsibility in the major legal systems of the world (England, United States, Germany, France, Denmark, Russia, China, and Islamic legal tradition), *Criminal Law Forum*, 2013, 24.P.28

[17] Brożek, B., Jakubiec, M. On the legal responsibility of autonomous machines, *Artificial Intelligence and Law*, 2017.

[18] Wallerstein S. Oblique intent in English and Jewish law, *Oxford Journal of Law and Religion*, 2014. 3(2), P. 258-285.

[19] Article 6, Rome Statute of the International Criminal Court, Text of the Rome Statute circulated as document A/CONF.183/9 of 17 July 1998 and corrected by process-verbaux of 10 November 1998, 12 July 1999, 30 November 1999, 8 May 2000, 17 January 2001 and 16 January 2002. The Statute entered into force on 1 July 2002. https://www.icc-cpi.int/NR/rdonlyres/EA9AEFF7-5752-4F84-BE94-0A655EB30E16/0/Rome_Statute_English.pdf

[20] AI programs exhibit racial and gender biases, research reveals, The Guardian, `https://www.theguardian.com/technology/2017/apr/13/ai-programs-exhibit-racist-and-sexist-biases-research-reveals`

[21] Caliskan A., Bryson J.J., Narayanan A. Semantics derived automatically from language corpora contain human-like biases, *Science*, 2017, 356(6334), P. 183-186.

[22] Article 6, Rome Statute of the International Criminal Court.

[23] New York Times, 25th March 2016, `https://www.nytimes.com/2016/03/25/technology/microsoft-created-a-twitter-bot-to-learn-from-users-it-quickly-became-a-racist-jerk.html`; The Telegraph, 24th March 2016, `https://www.telegraph.co.uk/technology/2016/03/24/microsofts-teen-girl-ai-turns-into-a-hitler-loving-sex-robot-wit/`

[24] Model Penal Code developed by the American Law Institute, `https://ia800102.us.archive.org/29/items/ModelPenalCode_ALI/MPC%20full%20%28504%20pages%29.pdf`

[25] Peter M. Asaro A Body to Kick, but Still No Soul to Damn: Legal Perspectives on Robotics in P.Lin, K. Abney and G. A. Bekey (eds.), Robot Ethics: The Ethical and Social Implications of Robotics, MIT Press, London, 2012. P.170.

[26] Peter M. Asaro A Body to Kick, but Still No Soul to Damn: Legal Perspectives on Robotics in P.Lin, K. Abney and G. A. Bekey (eds.), Robot Ethics: The Ethical and Social Implications of Robotics, MIT Press, London, 2012. P.172.

[27] Vellinga N.E. From the testing to the deployment of self-driving cars: Legal challenges to policymakers on the road ahead, *Computer Law and Security Review*, 2017, 33(6), P. 855.

[28] http://moralmachine.mit.edu/

[29] Article 7, The General Product Safety Regulations 2005, `http://www.legislation.gov.uk/uksi/2005/1803/regulation/7/made`

[30] Fenwick M. Corporate wrongdoing and the limits of the criminal law, P. 113 in «Facing the limits of the law», Publisher: Springer Berlin Heidelberg 2009.

[31] U.S. Code, Title 18, Part I, Chapter 44, § 930 «Possession of firearms and dangerous weapons in Federal facilities».

[32] U.S. Code, Title 18, Part I, Chapter 44, § 923 «Licensing».

[33] U.S. Code, Title 18, Part I, Chapter 44, § 922 «Unlawful acts»; US v Rene, 583 F.3d 8 (1st Cir. 2009), https://www.leagle.com/decision/infco20091005057.xml

[34] U.S. Constitution, Second Amendment.

[35] Bureau of Alcohol, Tobacco, Firearms and Explosives (ATF), https://www.atf.gov/

[36] Article 125, See for instance: https://www.cecc.gov/resources/legal-provisions/criminal-law-of-the-peoples-republic-of-china

[37] Article 226, The Criminal Code of The Russian Federation No. 63-FZ Of June 13, 1996, http://www.wipo.int/edocs/lexdocs/laws/en/ru/ru080en.pdf

[38] Criminal Law of the Peoples Republic of China, Section 7: crimes of smuggling, trafficking in, transporting and manufacturing narcotic drugs, http://www.fmprc.gov.cn/ce/cgvienna/eng/dbtyw/jdwt/crimelaw/t209043.html; Criminal Code of the Russian Federation, Articles 228-234, http://www.wipo.int/edocs/lexdocs/laws/en/ru/ru080en.pdf; Corruption, drug trafficking and other serious crimes (confiscation of benefits) act, (Chapter 65a), Singapore, https://sso.agc.gov.sg/Act/CDTOSCCBA1992; Sec. 60013 «Death penalty for gun murders during Federal crimes of violence and drug trafficking crimes» and TITLE X—«DRUG CONTROL», «Violent Crime Control and Law Enforcement Act of 1994» of the United States, http://legisworks.org/GPO/STATUTE-108-Pg1796.pdf etc.

[39] The world drug reports, UNDOC official site, http://www.unodc.org/doc/wdr2016/WORLD_DRUG_REPORT_2016_web.pdf

[40] U.S. Code, Title 18, Chapter 40 – «Importation, manufacture, distribution and storage of explosive materials», https://www.law.cornell.edu/uscode/text/18/part-I/chapter-40; Criminal Law of the Peoples Republic of China, Article 121, http://www.fmprc.gov.cn/ce/cgvienna/eng/dbtyw/jdwt/crimelaw/t209043.htm; Criminal Code of Russian Federation, Article 226. Stealing or Possession of Arms, Ammunition, Explosives, and Explosive Devices, http://www.wipo.int/edocs/lexdocs/laws/en/ru/ru080en.pdf

[41] Noel Sharkey Killing Made Easy: From Joysticks to Politics in P.Lin, K. Abney and G. A. Bekey (eds.), Robot Ethics: The Ethical and Social Implications of Robotics, MIT Press, London, 2012.P. 119.

[42] Vernick J.S. Carrying Guns in Public: Legal and Public Health Implications, *Journal of Law, Medicine and Ethics*, 2013. 41(SUPPL. 1), P. 85.

[43] Kosinski M., Wang Y. Deep neural networks are more accurate than humans at detecting sexual orientation from facial images, *Journal of Personality and Social Psychology*, 2018. 114(2), P. 246-257

[44] Youyou W., Kosinski M., Stillwell D. Computer-based personality judgments are more accurate than those made by humans, *Proceedings of the National Academy of Sciences of the United States of America*, 2015, 112(4), P. 1036-1040.

[45] Lay A., Ferwerda B. Predicting userspersonality based on their îikedîmages on Instagram, *CEUR Workshop Proceedings*, Volume 2068, 2018, 2018 Joint ACM IUI Workshops, ACMIUI-WS 2018; Celli F., Bruni E., Lepri B. Automatic personality and interaction style recognition from Facebook profile pictures, *MM 2014 - Proceedings of the 2014 ACM Conference on Multimedia*, 2014. pp. 1101-1104; Kaur A. Automatic personality assessment in the wild, *7th International Conference on Affective Computing and Intelligent Interaction*, ACII 2017, Volume 2018-January, 29 January 2018, Pages 586-590.

[46] Zhao L, Jia J., Feng L. Teenagers' stress detection based on time-sensitive micro-blog comment/response actions, *Artificial Intelligence in Theory and Practice IV*, 4th IFIP TC 12 International Conference on Artificial Intelligence, IFIP AI 2015, Held as Part of WCC 2015, Daejeon, South Korea, October 4-7, 2015, Proceedings. P. 26-35.

[47] https://www.independent.co.uk/news/world/asia/china-ai-crimes-before-happen-artificial-intelligence-security-plans-beijing-meng-jianzhu-a7962496.html

[48] Van der Sloot B.A new approach to the right to privacy, or how the European Court of Human Rights embraced the non-domination principle, *CComputer Law and Security Review*, 2018. 34(3), P. 539-549.

[49] Čerka P., Grigiene J., Sirbikyte G. Liability for damages caused by artificial intelligence, *Computer Law and Security Review*, 2015. 31(3), P. 376-389.

[50] Solum B. Lawrence Legal Personhood for Artificial Intelligences, *North Carolina Law Review*. Volume 70, Number 4, 1992. P. 1262.

[51] See for instance: Etzioni A., Etzioni O. Incorporating Ethics into Artificial Intelligence, *Journal of Ethics*, 21(4), 2017. P. 403-418; Asaro P. Robots and responsibility from a legal perspective. In: The IEEE conference on robotics and automation, 2007. http://www.peterasaro.org/writing/ASARO%20Legal%20Perspective.pdf; Danaher J. The rise of the robots and the crisis of moral patiency, *AI & Society*, 2017. P 1–8. https://link.springer.com/content/pdf/10.1007%2Fs00146-017-0773-9.pdf; Maldonato, M. Valerio, P.b

[52] See for instance: Koops B-J, Hildebrandt M, Jaquet-Chiffelle D-O (2010) Bridging the accountability gap: rights for new entities in the information

society, *Minnesota Journal of Law, Science & Technology*, Vol. 11, No 2, 2010. P. 497-561; Solaiman S.M. Legal personality of robots, corporations, idols and chimpanzees: a quest for legitimacy, *Artificial Intelligence and Law*, 25(2), 2017. P. 155-179; Bryson J.J., Diamantis M.E., Grant T.D. Of, for, and by the people: the legal lacuna of synthetic persons, *Artificial Intelligence and Law*, 25(3), 2017. P. 273-291;.

[53] See, for instance, website at NONHUMAN RTS. PROJECT, http:// www.nonhumanrightsproject.org; Staker A. Should Chimpanzees Have Standing? the Case for Pursuing Legal Personhood for Non-Human Animals, *Transnational Environmental Law*, 6(3), 2017, P. 485-507; Schmidt A.T. Persons or Property - Freedom and the Legal Status of Animals, *Journal of Moral Philosophy*, 15(1), 2018. P. 20-45.

[54] For instance, a judge in Argentina has recognized the female chimpanzee Cecilia as a legal person in Fraundorfer M. The Rediscovery of Indigenous Thought in the Modern Legal System: The Case of the Great Apes, *Global Policy*, 9(1), 2018. P. 17-25.

[55] Solaiman S.M. Legal personality of robots, corporations, idols and chimpanzees: a quest for legitimacy, *Artificial Intelligence and Law*, 25(2), 2017. P. 155-179;

[56] Draft Report of Committee on Legal Affairs (Rapporteur: Mady Delvaux) with recommendations to the Commission on Civil Law Rules on Robotics (2015/2103(INL)), http://www.europarl.europa.eu/sides/ getDoc.do?pubRef=-%2F%2FEP%2F%2FNONSGML%20COMPARL%20PE- 582.443%2001%20DOC%20PDF%20V0%2F%2FEN

[57] Bryson J.J., Diamantis M.E., Grant T.D. Of, for, and by the people: the legal lacuna of synthetic persons, *Artificial Intelligence and Law*, 2017. 25(3), P. 273-291.

[58] U.S. Department of Defense, Law of War Manual, 6.5.9.3 (2015), http://www.defense.gov/Portals/1/Documents/pubs/Law-of-War- Manual-June-2015.pdf.

[59] Bryson, P. 285.

[60] This manual reflects many years of labor and expertise, on the part of civilian and military lawyers from every Military Service. It reflects the experience of this Department in applying the law of war in actual military operations, and it will help us remember the hard learned lessons from the past. Understanding our duties imposed by the law of war and our rights under it is essential to our service in the nation's defense.

[61] See, for instance: Arato J. Subsequent Practice and Evolutive Interpretation: Techniques of Treaty Interpretation over Time and Their Diverse Consequences, *The Law and Practice of International Courts and Tribunals* 9 (2010) 443–494; Eirik Bjorge I. International Court of Justice, Case concerning the dispute regarding navigational and related rights (Costa Rica v

Nicaragua) judgment of 13 July 2009, *International and Comparative Law Quarterly*, 60, 2011. pp 271-279.

[62] Gabriel Hallevy, author of «Liability for crimes involving artificial intelligence systems», Publisher: Springer International Publishing, 2015 and other publications on this issue.

[63] Hallevy G., The Criminal Liability of Artificial Intelligence Entities, *SSRN Electronic Journal* (February 15, 2010). Available at SSRN: `https://ssrn.com/abstract=1564096` or `http://dx.doi.org/10.2139/ssrn.1564096`

[64] Halevy G. The criminal liability of artificial intelligence entities—from science fiction to legal social control, *Akron intellectual property journal*, Vol. 4 : Iss. 2, Article 1. Available at: `http://ideaexchange.uakron.edu/akronintellectualproperty/vol4/iss2/1194-199`.

[65] Hallevy G. Ibid. P. 197.

[66] See: Solaiman S.M. Legal personality of robots, corporations, idols and chimpanzees: a quest for legitimacy, *Artificial Intelligence and Law*, 25(2), 2017.

[67] Bryson, P.280.

[68] Everything You Need To Know About Sophia, The Worlds First Robot Citizen, Forbes Official site, `https://www.forbes.com/sites/zarastone/2017/11/07/everything-you-need-to-know-about-sophia-the-worlds-first-robot-citizen/`

[69] Bryson, P. 278.

[70] Sharlet R. Samizdat as a Source for the Study of Soviet Law, *Soviet and Post Soviet Review* (In 1974 the name of journal was Soviet Union), 1(1), 1974. P. 181-196

[71] Artificial sociability: from embodied AI toward new understandings of personhood, *Technology in Society*, 21, 1999. P. 385.

[72] Davenport D. Moral mechanisms, *Philosophy and Technology*, 27(1), 2014, P. 47-60.

[73] Staker A. Should Chimpanzees Have Standing? the Case for Pursuing Legal Personhood for Non-Human Animals, *Transnational Environmental Law*, 6(3), 2017, P. 494.

[74] Solum, P. 1286.

[75] Hallevy G. Liability for crimes involving artificial intelligence systems», Publisher: Springer International, 2015. P. 224.

[76] Fenwick M. Corporate wrongdoing and the limits of the criminal law, P. 112 in «Facing the limits of the law», Publisher: Springer Berlin Heidelberg 2009.

[77] Solaiman S.M. Legal personality of robots, corporations, idols and chimpanzees: a quest for legitimacy, *Artificial Intelligence and Law*, 25(2), 2017. P. 177.

[78] Buell S.W. The Responsibility Gap in Corporate Crime, *Criminal Law and Philosophy*, 2017. P. 1-21.

[79] Beck S. Intelligent agents and criminal law—Negligence, diffusion of liability and electronic personhood, *Robotics and Autonomous Systems*, 86, 2016. P. 138-143.

[80] Ahmedt-Aristizabal D., Fookes C., Nguyen K. Deep facial analysis: A new phase I epilepsy evaluation using computer vision, *Epilepsy and Behavior*, 82, 2018. P. 17-24; Zhou X., Jin K., Shang Y., Guo G. Visually Interpretable Representation Learning for Depression Recognition from Facial Images, *IEEE Transactions on Affective Computing*, 2018; Nithya, B., Ilango, V. Predictive analytics in health care using machine learning tools and techniques, *Proceedings of the 2017 International Conference on Intelligent Computing and Control Systems*, ICICCS 2017, 2018. 2018-January, P. 492-499.

[81] https://www.independent.co.uk/life-style/gadgets-and-tech/news/first-online-murder-will-happen-by-end-of-year-warns-us-firm-9774955.html

[82] Brenner S.W. At Light Speed: Attribution and Response to Cybercrime/Terrorism/Warfare, *Journal of Criminal Law and Criminology*, Vol. 97. No. 2, 2007. P.384.

[83] "Doxing is the intentional public release onto the Internet of personal information about an individual by a third party, often with the intent to humiliate, threaten, intimidate, or punish the identified individual" from Douglas D.M, Doxing: a conceptual analysis, *Ethics and Information Technology*, 18(3), 2016. P. 199.

[84] See for instance: Zhang Y., Gao H. Human Flesh Search Engine and Online Privacy, *Science and Engineering Ethics*, 22(2), 2016. P. 601-604.

[85] See for instance: Douglas D.M. Doxing: a conceptual analysis, *Ethics and Information Technology*, 18(3), 2016. P. 199.

[86] See for instance: cases described in Julia M. MacAllister, The Doxing Dilemma: Seeking a Remedy for the Malicious Publication of Personal Information, *Fordham Law Review*, Volume 85, Issue 5, (2017). Available at: http://ir.lawnet.fordham.edu/flr/vol85/iss5/21

[87] Khanna P., Zavarsky P., Lindskog D. Experimental Analysis of Tools Used for Doxing and Proposed New Transforms to Help Organizations Protect against Doxing Attacks, *Procedia Computer Science*, 94, 2016. P. 459-464.

[88] https://lyrebird.ai/; https://www.technologyreview.com/the-download/610386/a-new-algorithm-can-mimic-your-voice-with-just-snippets-of-audio/

[89] http://www.dailymail.co.uk/sciencetech/article-5463477/Baidus-creepy-new-AI-accurately-mimic-voice.html

[90] Judges R.A., Gallant S.N., Yang L., Lee, K. The role of cognition, personality, and trust in fraud victimization in older adults, *Frontiers in Psychology*, 8(APR), 588, 2017.

[91] https://www.fakeapp.org/;https://www.nytimes.com/2018/03/04/technology/fake-videos-deepfakes.html

[92] Stover D. Garlin Gilchrist: Fighting fake news and the information apocalypse, *Bulletin of the Atomic Scientists*, 74(4), 2018. P. 283-288.

[93] California Penal Code, Section 647 (3)(A) "Any person who uses a concealed camcorder, motion picture camera, or photographic camera of any type, to secretly videotape, film, photograph, or record by electronic means, another, identifiable person who may be in a state of full or partial undress, for the purpose of viewing the body of, or the undergarments worn by, that other person, without the consent or knowledge of that other person, in the interior of a bedroom, bathroom, changing room, fitting room, dressing room, or tanning booth, or the interior of any other area in which that other person has a reasonable expectation of privacy, with the intent to invade the privacy of that other person", http://law.onecle.com/california/penal/647.html

[94] Ryan D. European remedial coherence in the regulation of non-consensual disclosures of sexual images, *Computer Law and Security Review*, 2018. *https://www.sciencedirect.com/science/article/pii/S0267364918300475*

[95] https://www.gov.uk/government/uploads/system/uploads/attachment_data/file/666033/erratum-data.csv/preview

[96] Israel, Japan, Canada, Victoria in Australia, New Zealand and more than 30 states in the USA, information from McGlynn C., Rackley E. Image-based sexual abuse, *Oxford Journal of Legal Studies*, 37(3), 2017. P. 554.

[97] Marwick A.E. Scandal or sex crime? Gendered privacy and the celebrity nude photo leaks, *Ethics and Information Technology*, 19(3), 2017. P. 178.

[98] Deepfakes porn has serious consequences, https://www.bbc.com/news/technology-42912529

[99] Ryan D. European remedial coherence in the regulation of non-consensual disclosures of sexual images, *Computer Law and Security Review*, 2018. https://www.sciencedirect.com/science/article/pii/S0267364918300475

[100] Smith A. Nigerian scam e-mails and the charms of capital, *Cultural Studies*, 23(1), 2009. P. 28.

[101] Bergiel B.J., Bergiel E.B., Balsmeier P.W. Internet cross border crime: A growing problem, *Journal of Website Promotion*, 2008. 3(3-4), P. 133.

[102] Lecture of Oseledets Ivan, researcher of Skolkovo Institute of Science and Technology (Moscow, Russian Federation) that was held in Far Eastern Federal University, 18 July 2018.

[103] Mass murder in which a terrorist intentionally rams a motor vehicle into a crowd of people.

[104] From English abstract of Hauer T., Huschitt N., Klein F. Patient care after terrorist attacks: Experiences from the Berlin Christmas market attack (19 December 2016), *Notfall und Rettungsmedizin*, 21(4), 2018. P. 267-277.

[105] See for instance: Springer D.R., Regens J.L., Edger D.N. Islamic radicalism and global jihad, Publisher: Georgetown University Press, 2009. P. 133-144.

[106] Ibid, P. 135.

[107] Niu G., Chen Q. Learning an video frame-based face detection system for security fields, *Journal of Visual Communication and Image Representation*, 55, 2018. P. 457-463.

[108] El-Kaime H., Hanoune M., Eddaoui A. The Data Mining: A Solution for Credit Card Fraud Detection in Banking, *Advances in Intelligent Systems and Computing*, 756, 2019. P. 332-341

[109] Latha P.H., Vasantha R. An efficient security system in wireless local area network (WLAN) against network intrusion, *Advances in Intelligent Systems and Computing*, 763, 2019. P. 12-19.

[110] Issa H., Sun T., Vasarhelyi M.A. Research ideas for artificial intelligence in auditing: The formalization of audit and workforce supplementation, *Journal of Emerging Technologies in Accounting*, 13(2), 2016. P. 1-20.

[111] Dong Y., Su H., Zhu J., Zhang B. Improving interpretability of deep neural networks with semantic information, *Proceedings - 30th IEEE Conference on Computer Vision and Pattern Recognition*, CVPR, 2017-January, P. 975.

[112] Carrara F., Falchi F., Caldelli R., Amato G., Becarelli R. Adversarial image detection in deep neural networks, *Multimedia Tools and Applications*, 2018, P. 1-21. https://link.springer.com/article/10.10072Fs11042-018-5853-4

[113] Papernot N., McDaniel P., Goodfellow I. Practical black-box attacks against machine learning, *ASIA CCS 2017 - Proceedings of the 2017 ACM Asia Conference on Computer and Communications Security*, 2017. P. 506-519.

[114] Ibid, P. 2.

[115] Lizong Zhang, Zepeng Wang, A multi-view camera-based anti-fraud system and its applications, *Journal of Visual Communication and Image Representation*, Volume 55, August 2018, P. 263.

[116] Wicker M., Huang X., Kwiatkowska M. Feature-guided black-box safety testing of deep neural networks, *Lecture Notes in Computer Science 10805*, 2018. P. 409.

[117] Kevin Eykholt, Ivan Evtimov, Earlence Fernandes Robust Physical-World Attacks on Deep Learning Visual Classification, *CVPR 2018*, 2018. https://arxiv.org/pdf/1707.08945.pdf

[118] Rowley J., Liu A., Sandry S. Examining the driverless future: An analysis of human-caused vehicle accidents and development of an autonomous vehicle communication testbed, *Systems and Information Engineering Design Symposium*, SIEDS 2018 , 2018. P. 58-63.

[119] What to Think About Machines That Think: Todays Leading Thinkers on the Age of Machine Intelligence (Edge Question). Edited by John Brockman, Publisher: New York : Harper Perennial, 2015. 576 p.

[120] The Merriam-Webster Dictionary, "Definition: Anthropomorphize," Date unavailable, https://www.merriam-webster.com/dictionary/anthropomorphize

[121] Nicholas Epley, Adam Waytz, and John T. Cacioppo, On seeing human: A three-factor theory of anthropomorphism, *Psychological Review* (2007): vol. 114, no. 4, pp. 864-886.

[122] Epley, Waytz, and Cacioppo, On seeing human, *Psychological Review*, p. 877.

[123] Epley, Waytz, and Cacioppo, On seeing human, *Psychological Review*, p. 879.

[124] Clive Thompson, The secret history of women in coding, *The New York Times*, February 13th, 2019, https://www.nytimes.com/2019/02/13/magazine/women-coding-computer-programming.html

[125] Mark West, Rebecca Kraut, and Han Ei Chew, "I'd Blush if I Could: Closing gender divides in digital skills through education," UNESCO, 2019, https://unesdoc.unesco.org/ark:/48223/pf0000367416.page=1

[126] The World Bank, "Population, female (% of total) in 2017," *The World Bank Data*, 2019, https://data.worldbank.org/indicator/sp.pop.totl.fe.zs

[127] Dieter Bohn, "Amazon says 100 million Alexa devices have been sold – what's next?", *The Verge*, January 4th, 2019, https://www.theverge.com/2019/1/4/18168565/amazon-alexa-devices-how-many-sold-number-100-million-dave-limp

[128] Russell Holly, "Microsoft says Cortana now has more than 141 million monthly users", *Windows Central*, May 10th, 2017, `https://www.windowscentral.com/cortana-now-has-over-141-million-users-every-month`

[129] Jilian D'Onfro, "Google's small hardware business is shaping up, could book $20 billion in sales by 2021, RBC says," *CNBC*, December 21st, 2018, `https://www.cnbc.com/2018/12/21/google-hardware-revenue-profit-potential-rbc-analyst-mark-mahaney.html`

[130] Dieter Bohn, "Google Assistant will soon be on a billion devices, and feature phones are next", *The Verge*, January 7th, 2019, `https://www.theverge.com/2019/1/7/18169939/google-assistant-billion-devices-feature-phones-ces-2019`

[131] Ava Mutchler, "Apple Announces Update to Siri at WWDC, Claims 375 Million Monthly Active Users", *Voicebot.ai*, June 6th, 2017, `https://voicebot.ai/2017/06/06/apple-announces-update-siri-wwdc-claims-375-million-monthly-active-users/`

[132] Leah Fessler, "We tested bots like Siri and Alexa to see who would stand up to sexual harassment", *Quartz*, February 22nd, 2017, `https://qz.com/911681/we-tested-apples-siri-amazon-echos-alexa-microsofts-cortana-and-googles-google-home-to-see-which-personal-assistant-bots-stand-up-for-themselves-in-the-face-of-sexual-harassment/`

[133] Dalia Mortada "Meet Q, the first gender-neutral voice assistant", *NPR*, March 21st, 2019, `https://www.genderlessvoice.com`

[134] Jenny W. Hsu, "Alibaba gives 'sight' to its smart speaker", *Alizila*, March 26th, 2018, `https://www.alizila.com/alibaba-gives-sight-smart-speaker/`

[135] David H. Autor. Why are there still so many jobs? the history and future of workplace automation. *Journal of Economic Perspectives*, 29(3):3–30, 2015.

[136] Stephen J DeCanio. Robots and humans–complements or substitutes? *Journal of Macroeconomics*, 49:280–291, 2016.

[137] Michael Decker, Martin Fischer, and Ingrid Ott. Service robotics and human labor: A first technology assessment of substitution and cooperation. *Robotics and Autonomous Systems*, 87:348–354, 2017.

[138] Cüneyt Dirican. The impacts of robotics, artificial intelligence on business and economics. *Procedia-Social and Behavioral Sciences*, 195:564–573, 2015.

[139] Horst Feldmann. Technological unemployment in industrial countries. *Journal of Evolutionary Economics*, 23(5):1099–1126, 2013.

[140] Ruosi LU. Labor market segregation and the wage differential between resident and migrant workers in china. 2008.

[141] Margaret E Madden, Marsha Baxter, Heather Beauchamp, Kimberley Bouchard, Derek Habermas, Mark Huff, Brian Ladd, Jill Pearon, and Gordon Plague. Rethinking stem education: An interdisciplinary steam curriculum. *Procedia Computer Science*, 20:541–546, 2013.

[142] Xin Meng and Junsen Zhang. The two-tier labor market in urban china: occupational segregation and wage differentials between urban residents and rural migrants in shanghai. *Journal of comparative Economics*, 29(3):485–504, 2001.

[143] Mohammed Owais Qureshi and Rumaiya Sajjad Syed. The impact of robotics on employment and motivation of employees in the service sector, with special reference to health care. *Safety and health at work*, 5(4):198–202, 2014.

[144] Daniel Susskind et al. A model of technological unemployment. *University of Oxford, Department of Economics Discussion Paper.* https://www.economics.ox.ac.uk/materials/papers/15126/819-susskind-a-model-of-technological-unemploymentjuly-2017.pdf, 2017.

[145] Philip Brook Manville, The Origins of Citizenship in Ancient Athens, Princeton University Press, 2014, pp. 3–34.

[146] Alister McGrath nicely captures the role of the Church for salvation in the pre-Luther era: "An individual's hope of salvation rested on her being part of the community of saints, whose visible expression was the institution of the church. The church could not be bypassed or marginalized in any account of redemption: there was, as Cyprian of Carthage had so cogently argued in the third century, no salvation outside the church", *Luther's Theology of the Cross: Martin Luther's Theological Breakthrough*, 2nd ed. Malden, MA: Wiley-Blackwell, 2011, p. 12).

[147] For more discussion about the relationship between Luther's reform and individualism, see Louis Dumont, "A Modified View of Our Origins: The Christian Beginnings of Modern Individualism", *Contributions to Indian Sociology*, 17, no. 1 (1983): 1–26.

[148] While the well-known Latin formulation "cogito, ergo sum" is taken from Descartes's *Principles of Philosophy*, the idea was first expressed in French in *Discourse on the Method* as "je pense, donc je suis". See René Descartes, *Œuvres de Descartes*, vol. 7, ed. C. Adam and P. Tannery, Paris: J. Vrin, 1996, p. 32.

[149] The famous phrase "God is dead" occurs multiple times in Friedrich Wilhelm Nietzsche, *The Gay Science: With a Prelude in German Rhyme and an Appendix of Song*, trans. J. Nauckhoff and A. Del Caro, Cambridge University Press, 2001, pp. 108, 125, 343.

[150] See, for example, Friedrich Wilhelm Nietzsche, *Twilight of the Idols with the Antichrist and Ecce Homo*, trans. Judith Norma (Ware, UK: Wordsworth Editions, 2007), p. 5.

[151] Many of Nietzsche's commentators suggest the same interpretation for Nietzsche's view concerning the origin of Christianity, which is to promote certain social functions. For example, see Julian Yong, *Nietzsche's Philosophy of Religion* (Cambridge: Cambridge University Press, 2006), pp. 151–152. Karl Marx and Friedrich Engels, *On Religion*, trans. Foreign Languages Publication House (Moscow: Institut Marksizma-Leninizma, 1957), p. 42.

[152] Kathleen Freeman, *Ancill to the Pre-Socrati Philosophers: A Complete Translation of the Fragments in Diels*, Fragments der Vorsokratiker (Cambridge, MA: Harvard University Press, 1996), pp. 157–158 (88B25).

[153] Jared Diamond famously argues that religion enables tribal societies to organize themselves into larger political institutions, thus explaining why religion is usually found in large social units but not hunter-gatherer ones: "Besides justifying the transfer of wealth to kleptocrats, institutionalized religion brings two other important benefits to centralized societies. First, shared ideology or religion helps solve the problem of how unrelated individuals are to live together without killing each other—by providing them with a bond not based on kinship. Second, it gives people a motive, other than genetic self-interest, for sacrificing their lives on behalf of others. At the cost of a few society members who die in battle as soldiers, the whole society becomes much more effective at conquering other societies or resisting attacks", Guns, Germs and Steel: A Short History of Everybody for the Last 13,000 years [New York: Random House, 1998], p. 278).

[154] For detailed arguments in favor of an adaptive explanation of religion, see Scott Atran, *In Gods We Trust: The Evolutionary Landscape of Religion.* (Oxford: Oxford University Press, 2004).

[155] Many historians refer to this period of instability during the French Revolution as the "Reign of Terror." For a more detailed historical introduction, see *"Reign of Terror"*, Encyclopedia Britannica, December 18, 2017, available at `https://www.britannica.com/event/Reign-of-Terror` (accessed July 25, 2018).

[156] An insightful analysis of the dynamics can be found in *"Absolute Freedom and Terror"* by Georg Wilhelm Friedrich Hegel, *The Phenomenology of Spirit*, trans. Terry Pinkard (Cambridge: Cambridge University Press, 2018), pp. 339–347.

[157] Another proponent of utilitarianism, J. S. Mill, puts the principle as follows: "The creed which accepts as the foundation of morals, Utility, or the Greatest-Happiness Principle, holds that actions are right in proportion as they tend to promote happiness, wrong as they tend to produce the reverse of happiness. By happiness is intended pleasure, and the absence of

pain; by unhappiness, pain, and the privation of pleasure" in *Utilitarianism*, Chicago University Press, 1906, p. 9.

[158] See Jeremy Bentham, *The Panopticon Writings*, ed. Miran Božovič (London: Verso, 1995), p. 1.

[159] Bentham, *The Panopticon Writings*, ed. Miran Božovivc (London: Verso, 1995), p. 35.

[160] Bentham, *The Panopticon Writings*, ed. Miran Božovič (London: Verso, 1995), p. 43.

[161] Bentham, *The Panopticon Writings*, ed. Miran Božovič (London: Verso, 1995), p. 45.

[162] Bentham, *The Panopticon Writings*, ed. Miran Božovič (London: Verso, 1995), p. 29.

[163] Bentham, *The Panopticon Writings*, ed. Miran Božovič (London: Verso, 1995), p. 33-34.

[164] Bentham, *The Panopticon Writings*, ed. Miran Božovič (London: Verso, 1995), p. 31.

[165] Michel Foucault, *Discipline and Punish: The Birth of the Prison*, trans. Alan Sheridan (New York: Vintage Books, 1995), p. 202.

[166] Foucault, *Discipline and Punish*, p. 222.

[167] Shoshana Zuboff, *In the Age of the Smart Machine: The Future of Work and Power*. New York: Basic Books, 198), p. 322.

[168] Claude Castelluccia provides a nice categorization and functional description for different behavioral tracking models adopted by large technological companies. Included in the categories are web tracking, location tracking, and social network tracking. For detailed examples and characterizations, see Claude Castelluccia, "Behavioural Tracking on the Internet: A Technical Perspective," in *European Data Protection: In Good Health?*, ed. S. Gutwirth et al. (Dordrecht: Springer, 2012), pp. 21–33.

[169] Emotional AI has been a prosperous research area to which many technology companies are devoted. In a recent paper published on the topic of informational privacy policy, Sedenburg and Chuang reported that "recently, Facebook has been under scrutiny for patents that enable computer and cell phone cameras to detect emotion of users while using the site so that platform content (peer-generated and advertising) can be tailored for the individual." See Elaine Sedenburg and John Chuang, "Smile for the Camera: Privacy and Policy Implications of Emotion AI", *Computing Research Repository*, ~arXiv:\1709.00396~, 2017.

[170] For example, see Greg Conti, *Googling Security: How Much Does Google Know About You?* (Boston: Addison-Wesley, 2009).

[171] By running a series of experiments, Emilee Radar investigated the extent to which Internet users are aware of the capacities Facebook and Google possess to infer users' behavioral and psychological characters, including sensitive information about their sexual orientation. She concludes as follows: "This paper shows that users' perceptions about what unwanted access looks like have very little resemblance to the actual ability of personalization and advertising algorithms to make inferences about them, and this problem will only grow as networked sensors (and the efficiencies and conveniences they provide) become more integrated in our daily activities." See E. Radar, "Awareness of Behavioral Tracking and Information Privacy Concern in Facebook and Google," paper presented at the *Symposium on Usable Privacy and Security (SOUPS)*, Menlo Park, CA, July 2014.

[172] Computer science researchers at Princeton University confirmed that many Google services on Android devices and iPhones store users' precise location data — latitude and longitude accurate to the square foot — even if the user has chosen a privacy setting that does not allow Google to do so (Ryan Nakashima, "Google Tracks your Movements, Like It or Not", Associated Press News, August 14, 2018, available at `https://apnews.com/828aefab64d4411bac257a07c1af0ecb` [accessed August 15, 2018]).

[173] One of the most controversial privacy-infringing features of Facebook is its advertisement system Beacon, which tracks users' actions on third-party websites that are partnered with Facebo ok, even when the user is off-line. When the feature was first introduced in 2007, Facebook did not e-mail the Beacon announcement to its users, nor did it take any other additional measures to notify its users of the new product. For more discussions of the privacy-infringing features of Facebook, see Yasamine Hashemi, "Facebook's Privacy Policy and Its Third-Party Partnerships: Lucrativity and Liability", *Boston University Journal of Science and Technology*, 15 (2009): 140.

[174] Alix Langone, "Facebook Admits It May Collect Data About Your Calls and Text Messages. Here's How to Turn It Off",' *Time*, March 26, 2018, available at `http://time.com/5215274/facebook-messenger-android-call-text-message-data` (accessed July 22, 2018).

[175] In reviewing the ways in which Internet users' behavior is tracked and precautionary measures one could take to avoid privacy infringement, Castelluccia suggests that "there is no easy way to use modern, cookie- and Java Script-dependent web sites and social networking sites and avoid tracking at the same time" ("Behavioural Tracking on the Internet", pp. 21–33). Some scholars even argue that withdrawal from the online world is the only method to secure privacy. For example, as Conti puts it, "short of abstinence, no clear solution exists for protecting yourself and your company from web-based information disclosure" (Googling Security, chap. 9).

[176] Carole Cadwalladr and Emma Graham-Harrison, "Revealed: 50 Million Facebook Profiles Harvested for Cambridge Analytica in Ma-

jor Data Breach', *The Guardian*, March 17, 2018, available at `https://www.theguardian.com/news/2018/mar/17/cambridge-analytica-facebook-influence-us-election` (accessed August 8, 2018).

[177] In May 2013, former CIA employee Edward Snowden disclosed to *The Guardian*, a British newspaper, approximately 1.7 million documents of secret data from the NSA, exposing the mass surveillance programs conducted on average US citizens, foreign leaders, and various other targets worldwide. The incident triggered an immediate outcry concerning government surveillance in the age of citizens' information transparency. For detailed discussion of the incident, see Joseph Verble, "The NSA and Edward Snowden: Surveillance in the 21st Century", *ACM SIGCAS Computers and Society* 44, no. 3 (2014): 14–20.

[178] As of 2018, China ranked the fifth worst among 180 counties in the World Press Freedom Index, a measurement of the degree of severity of Internet and press censorship by governments across the world, as conducted by Reporters Without Borders: "2018 World Press Freedom Index," available at `https://rsf.org/en/ranking` (accessed July 23, 2018).

[179] "The Great Firewall" is only a part of the surveillance project officially titled the "Golden Shield Project". See Greg Walton, China's Golden Shield: Corporations and the Development of Surveillance Technology in the People's Republic of China (Montreal: Rights and Democracy, 2001), pp. 15–17. For technical investigation of how the Great Firewall blocks international websites such as Google and Facebook, see Guangchao Charles Feng and Steve Zhongshi Guo, "Tracing the Route of China's Internet Censorship: An Empirical Study", *Telematics and Informatics*, 30, no. 4 (2013): 335–345.

[180] For technical discussions about how the Chinese government takes down content from the Internet and social media, see David Bamman, Brendan O'Connor, and Noah A. Smith, "Censorship and Deletion Practices in Chinese Social Media", *First Monday*, 17, no. 3 (2012).

[181] In March 2012, Beijing Municipality issued new regulations requiring social media in China, like Sina and other microblog hosting companies, to implement a real-name registration system. User account suspensions in social media are therefore directly affiliated with regulations on the user's off-line activities. For case studies of user account suspensions, see Johan Lagerkvist, "Principal-Agent Dilemma in China's Social Media Sector? The Party-State and Industry Real-Name Registration Waltz", *International Journal of Communication*, 6 (2012): 2628–2646.

[182] For further discussions about the motivations and consequence of the Cybersecurity Law, see Mark Parasol, "The Impact of China's 2016 Cyber Security Law on Foreign Technology Firms, and on China's Big Data and Smart City Dreams", *Computer Law & Security Review*, 34 (2018): 67–98.

[183] China has the world's largest volume of mobile payments, totaling 81
trillion yuan (about US$12.77 trillion) as of October 2017: "Global
and China Mobile Payment Industry Report, 2017–2021", available
at `https://www.researchandmarkets.com/research/q2gr6q/global_`
`and_china?w=12` (accessed July 23, 2018).

[184] Josh Chin and Liza Lin, "China's All-Seeing Surveillance State Is Reading
Its Citizens' Faces", *Wall Street Journal*, June 26, 2017, available at
`https://www.wsj.com/articles/the-all-seeing-surveillance-`
`state-feared-in-the-west-is-a-reality-in-china-1498493020`
(accessed August 8, 2018).

[185] A BBC reporter (John Sudworth) who tested CCTV facial recognition managed to travel anonymously in the city of Guiyang for only
seven minutes before he was spotted by the CCTV facial recognition and caught by security officers. See Joyce Liu, "In Your Face:
China's All-Seeing State", BBC News, December 10, 2017, available at `https://www.bbc.com/news/av/world-asia-china-42248056/`
`in-your-face-china-s-all-seeing-state` (accessed July 23, 2018).

[186] Rogier Creemers, "China's Social Credit System: An Evolving Practice of
Control", *Social Science Research Network*, May 9, 2018, available at `http:`
`//dx.doi.org/10.2139/ssrn.3175792` (accessed August 8, 2018).

[187] Celia Hatton, "China 'Social Credit': Beijing Sets Up Huge System",
BBC News, October 26, 2015, available at `https://www.bbc.com/news/`
`world-asia-china-34592186` (accessed July 23, 2018).

[188] Martin Chorzempa, Paul Triolo, and Samm Sacks, "China's Social Credit
System: A Mark of Progress or a Threat to Privacy?" (Washing-
ton, DC: *Peterson Institute for International Economics*, 2018), available
at `https://piie.com/publications/policy-briefs/chinas-social-`
`credit-system-mark-progress-or-threat-privacy` (accessed July 23,
2018).

[189] Zuboff, In the Age of the Smart Machine, p. 323.

[190] Zuboff, In the Age of the Smart Machine, p. 349.

[191] Many researchers report a lax attitude of users toward privacy-infringing
policies due to the gratification brought by the usage of the concerned media, despite their knowledge of the privacy problem. For example, see Bern-
hard Debatin and Jennette P. Lovejoy, "Facebook and Online Privacy: Attitudes, Behaviors, and Unintended Consequences", *Journal of Computer-
Mediated Communication*, 15 (2009): 83–108.

[192] Zuboff, In the Age of the Smart Machine, p. 351.

[193] As far as the currently available human prediction abilities are concerned, it is at least certain that "computer personality judgments have higher external validity when predicting life outcomes such as substance use, political attitudes, and physical health; for some outcomes, they even outperform the self-rated personality scores" (Youyou Wu, Michal Kosinski, and David Stillwell, "Computer-Based Personality Judgments Are More Accurate Than Those Made by Humans", *Proceedings of the National Academy of Sciences*, 112, no. 4 [2015]: 1036).

[194] This situation is nicely captured by a statement made by Scott McNealy, CEO and founder of Sun Microsystems: "You already have zero privacy—get over it," quoted in Robert Scheer, "Nowhere to Hide," Yahoo Internet Life (Special Report on Privacy) 6, no. 10 (2000): 101.

[195] Francis Fukuyama, "The End of History?', 'em The National Interest, 16 (1989): 4.

[196] "It is my hypothesis that the fundamental source of conflict in this new world will not be primarily ideological or primarily economic. The great divisions among humankind and the dominating source of conflict will be cultural. Nation-states will remain the most powerful actors in world affairs, but the principal conflicts of global politics will occur between nations and groups of different civilizations. The clash of civilizations will dominate global politics. The fault lines between civilizations will be the battle lines of the future" (Samuel P. Huntington, "The Clash of Civilizations?", *Foreign Affairs*, 72, no. 3 [Summer 1993]: 22).

[197] Kimiko de Freytas-Tamura, "What's Next for Humanity: Automation, New Morality and a 'Global Useless Class'", *The New York Times*, March 19, 2018, available at `https://www.nytimes.com/2018/03/19/world/europe/yuval-noah-harari-future-tech.html` (accessed November 3, 2018).

[198] De Freytas-Tamura, "What's Next for Humanity".

[199] Yuval Noah Harari, Homo Deus: A Brief History of Tomorrow (London: Harvill Secker, 2016), p. 345.

[200] Yuval Noah Harari, Homo Deus: A Brief History of Tomorrow (London: Harvill Secker, 2016), p. 385. According to Harari, "Dataism was born from the explosive confluence of two scientific tidal waves. In the 150 years since Charles Darwin published On the Origin of Species, the life sciences have come to see organisms as biochemical algorithms. Simultaneously, in the eight decades since Alan Turing formulated the idea of a Turing Machine, computer scientists have learned to engineer increasingly sophisticated electronic algorithms. Dataism puts the two together, pointing out that exactly the same mathematical laws apply to both biochemical and electronic algorithms. Dataism thereby collapses the barrier between animals and machines, and expects electronic algorithms to eventually decipher and outperform biochemical algorithms" (Harari, Homo Deus, p. 367).

[201] Yuval Noah Harari, Homo Deus: A Brief History of Tomorrow (London: Harvill Secker, 2016), p. 387.

[202] Yuval Noah Harari, Homo Deus: A Brief History of Tomorrow (London: Harvill Secker, 2016), p. 389.

[203] Yuval Noah Harari, Homo Deus: A Brief History of Tomorrow (London:

[204] Philip Adler, Casey Falk, Sorelle A. Friedler, Tionney Nix, Gabriel Ry-beck, Carlos Scheidegger, Brandon Smith, and Suresh Venkatasubrama-nian. Auditing black-box models for indirect influence. *Knowl. Inf. Syst.*, 54(1):95–122, 2018.

[205] Common Criteria Recognition Arrangement. The common criteria. https://www.commoncriteriaportal.org/. [Online; accessed in 2018].

[206] BBC News. Artificial intelligence: Google's AlphaGo beats Go master Lee Se-dol. https://www.bbc.com/news/technology-35785875, 2016. [Online; accessed in 2018].

[207] Nicholas Carlini and David Wagner. Adversarial examples are not easily detected: Bypassing ten detection methods. In *Proceedings of the 10th ACM Workshop on Artificial Intelligence and Security*, AISec '17, pages 3–14. ACM, 2017.

[208] Chih-Hong Cheng, Georg Nührenberg, Chung-Hao Huang, and Harald Ruess. Verification of binarized neural networks via inter-neuron factor-ing. In *Working Conference on Verified Software: Theories, Tools, and Ex-periments*, 2018.

[209] Nilesh Dalvi, Pedro Domingos, Mausam, Sumit Sanghai, and Deepak Verma. Adversarial classification. In *Proceedings of the Tenth ACM SIGKDD International Conference on Knowledge Discovery and Data Mining*, pages 99–108. ACM, 2004.

[210] Cynthia Dwork. Differential privacy: A survey of results. In Manindra Agrawal, Dingzhu Du, Zhenhua Duan, and Angsheng Li, editors, *Theory and Applications of Models of Computation*, pages 1–19, 2008.

[211] European Commission. Artificial Intelligence for Europe. http://ec.europa.eu/newsroom/dae/document.cfm?doc_id=51625, 2018. [Online; accessed in 2018].

[212] Kevin Eykholt, Ivan Evtimov, Earlence Fernandes, Bo Li, Amir Rahmati, Chaowei Xiao, Atul Prakash, Tadayoshi Kohno, and D. Song. Robust physical-world attacks on deep learning visual classification. In *Confer-ence on Computer Vision and Pattern Recognition*, 2018.

[213] Sorelle A. Friedler, Carlos Scheidegger, and Suresh Venkatasubramanian. On the (im)possibility of fairness. *CoRR*, abs/1609.07236, 2016.

[214] Ian Goodfellow, Jonathon Shlens, and Christian Szegedy. Explaining and harnessing adversarial examples. In *International Conference on Learning Representations*, 2015.

[215] Jim Hearn. Does the common criteria paradigm have a future? *IEEE Security & Privacy*, 2(1):64–65, 2004.

[216] Ling Huang, Anthony D. Joseph, Blaine Nelson, Benjamin I.P. Rubinstein, and J. D. Tygar. Adversarial machine learning. In *Proceedings of the 4th ACM Workshop on Security and Artificial Intelligence*, AISec '11, pages 43–58. ACM, 2011.

[217] Xiaowei Huang, Marta Kwiatkowska, Sen Wang, and Min Wu. Safety verification of deep neural networks. In *Computer Aided Verification*, pages 3–29, 2017.

[218] Guy Katz, Clark Barrett, David L. Dill, Kyle Julian, and Mykel J. Kochenderfer. Reluplex: An efficient smt solver for verifying deep neural networks. In *Computer Aided Verification*, pages 97–117, 2017.

[219] Pang Wei Koh and Percy Liang. Understanding black-box predictions via influence functions. In *International Conference on Machine Learning*, 2017.

[220] Vijay Kumar. Irrational Exuberance and the 'FATE' of Technology. https://cacm.acm.org/blogs/blog-cacm/230472-irrational-exuberance-and-the-fate-of-technology/fulltext, 2018. [Online; accessed in 2018].

[221] Tom M. Mitchell. The need for biases in learning generalizations. In Jude W. Shavlik and Thomas G. Dietterich, editors, *Readings in Machine Learning*, pages 184–191. Morgan Kauffman, 1980.

[222] Nina Narodytska, Shiva Prasad Kasiviswanathan, Leonid Ryzhyk, Mooly Sagiv, and Toby Walsh. Verifying properties of binarized deep neural networks. In *AAAI Conference on Artificial Intelligence*, 2018.

[223] Marco Tulio Ribeiro, Sameer Singh, and Carlos Guestrin. "why should i trust you?": Explaining the predictions of any classifier. In *SIGKDD International Conference on Knowledge Discovery and Data Mining*, pages 1135–1144. ACM, 2016.

[224] David Silver, Aja Huang, Chris J. Maddison, Arthur Guez, Laurent Sifre, George van den Driessche, Julian Schrittwieser, Ioannis Antonoglou, Veda Panneershelvam, Marc Lanctot, Sander Dieleman, Dominik Grewe, John Nham, Nal Kalchbrenner, Ilya Sutskever, Timothy Lillicrap, Madeleine Leach, Koray Kavukcuoglu, Thore Graepel, and Demis Hassabis. Mastering the game of Go with deep neural networks and tree search. *Nature*, 529(7587):484–489, 2016.

[225] David Silver, Julian Schrittwieser, Karen Simonyan, Ioannis Antonoglou, Aja Huang, Arthur Guez, Thomas Hubert, Lucas Baker, Matthew Lai,

Adrian Bolton, Yutian Chen, Timothy Lillicrap, Fan Hui, Laurent Sifre, George van den Driessche, Thore Graepel, and Demis Hassabis. Mastering the game of go without human knowledge. *Nature*, 550:354–359, 2017.

[226] Michael Skirpan and Micha Gorelick. The authority of "fair" in machine learning. In *Workshop on Fairness, Accountability, and Transparency in Machine Learning*, 2017.